COMING HOME

FRED M. WOOD

BROADMAN PRESS
Nashville, Tennessee

© Copyright 1987 ● Broadman Press
    All Rights Reserved
    4212-36
ISBN: 0-8054-1236-0
Dewey Decimal Classification: 224.1
Subject Heading: BIBLE O.T. ISAIAH 40-55
Library of Congress Catalog Number: 86-20775
Printed in the United States of America

Library of Congress Cataloging-in-Publication Data

Wood, Fred M.
  Coming home.

  1. Bible. O.T. Isaiah XL-LV—Commentaries.
I. Bible. O.T. Isaiah. II. Title.
BS1520.W67 1987   224'.107   86-20775
ISBN 0-8054-1236-0

Affectionately dedicated to
Dr. and Mrs. Dillard West
and
Mr. and Mrs. Willard Smith,
parents of our daughters-in-law
Glenda and Ginny

Contents

Preface:
A Word About the Prophet

How many "Isaiahs" were there? Years ago I heard a story—which at this moment I cannot document—about Dwight L. Moody, the itinerant evangelist, and George Adam Smith, the brilliant professor from Aberdeen, Scotland. According to the story, Moody invited Smith to come to America to help him in some revival meetings. Smith replied, "You don't want me. I believe in two and perhaps three Isaiahs." Moody said, "Come on. The people you'll be preaching to haven't even heard of one Isaiah."

Southern Baptists have mostly held to one author for the entire sixty-six chapters. Some, however, have studied Isaiah and have accepted a Deutero Isaiah, with the first authoring chapters 1—39 and the second authoring chapters 40—66. An even smaller number have accepted a Trito Isaiah, with the division being chapters 1—39; 40—55; 56—66. A few Southern Baptists have examined the question and have concluded that we can't be certain. They feel the same way as a man of intellectual integrity who said, "It matters not with which pen the king writes his message so long as it be true that the king wrote the message." One of the glorious things about living under the Lordship of Christ is that we have the right to choose for ourselves concerning matters such as these.

Chapters 1—39 definitely come from the ministry of Isaiah who preached in Jerusalem and Judah from 740 BC to shortly after 701 BC. Beginning with chapter 40, however, the scene changes abruptly. No longer is the prophet warning that the nation will be punished by being sent into Exile. Rather, they are in captivity in Babylon and, after having served as slaves for a number of years, are about to return home. The question is: Was Isaiah of Jerusalem, in his latter years, inspired by God's Spirit to compose the great masterpiece we find in chapters 40—66, or did a prophet in Babylon where the Jews were captive deliver and record them, under the leadership of God's Spirit, shortly before the Jews came back home about 535 BC?

The "Trito Isaiah" school of thought contends that chapters 40—55 were from a "Deutero Isaiah." A third person then picked up at chapter 56, after the Jews had arrived back home, and continued the message through chapter 66, the end of the book.

I certainly believe that God is quite capable of inspiring a man to write a great symphonic drama about events that will take place 150 years later. On the other hand, I know many sincere Bible students who simply do not believe it was done that way but insist on a Deutero Isaiah and even a Trito Isaiah. The only thing I suggest is that one should study the question thoroughly before trying to anathematize a fellow Christian for holding a position different from one's own.

Now you see the dilemma I face in this book on Isaiah 40—55. If I call the spokesman "Deutero Isaiah," those who believe in only one Isaiah will "fall out" with me. However, if I call him "Isaiah," many who believe in the Deutero and Trito Isaiah will forsake me.

What can I do? At the risk of losing both groups, I am simply going to call him "the prophet." Whichever view you take, you can read your own position into the expression. I hope you will let me use this designation and not accuse me of being a compromiser or a "fence straddler." After all, whoever delivered the messages in chapters 40—55 was certainly a prophet.

1
Than Which There Is No Greater
(40:1-31)

The Exile was over! When Hezekiah showed the envoys of Merodach-baladan, king of Babylon, all his treasures and those of the nation, Isaiah warned him the day would come when that nation whose time had not yet arrived would plunder the royal house and take his descendants captive. With a Louis-XIV attitude of *apres moi, le deluge,* the king said flippantly, "Good is the word . . . For there shall be peace and truth in my day" (Isa. 39:8).

That Exile came, but now it was over! If we count the beginning of the Babylonian captivity from the first invasion of Jerusalem in 605 BC when Nebuchadnezzar took the first group of Israelites captive, Jeremiah's seventy years of captivity prediction was fulfilled in 535 BC when the first group of exiles left Babylon on their return to the city. If we start from the destruction of the Temple in 586 BC, the seventy years would be fulfilled when the newly built Temple was dedicated in 516 BC.

Chapters 40—55 of Isaiah are couched against the background of Israel's return home! Like a great symphony, several themes recur as the majestic message swells with a crescendo that surpasses any melodious outburst found elsewhere in prophetic literature. At the forefront of this literary and spiritual masterpiece is an overture that sets forth the basic tenet of Hebrew faith. God reigns, and nothing or no one can usurp His claim nor cause Him to abdicate control of the natural forces present in His universe or His climactic creation: humankind. As a medieval theologian said, "God is that than which there is no greater!"

What is the dominant theme of this great prophetic message? Traditionally, "the salvation of the Lord" stands as the basic thrust, but actually a closer study reveals a greater truth set forth. Although the prophet declared strikingly that the long-promised deliverance was almost a reality, he dealt with another even more important issue. Why

9

had Israel been saved? If he had taught that the nation survived the
political revolutions of the eighth, seventh, and sixth centuries merely to
move by a cosmic stroke of power into the place of leadership held by
Assyria in the past, Babylon in the present, and Persia in the near future,
his message would be so irrelevant it would not be worth a moment's
consideration.

Why did God choose Abraham in the first place? Not to glorify a
people but to acquire an instrument for worldwide redemption. Abraham's greatest honor would not be his physical descendants but his
spiritual ones! Paul said it clearly, "He saith not, And to seeds, as of
many; but as of one, And to thy seed, which is Christ" (Gal. 3:16).
Sometimes bluntly, often subtly, but always implicitly, the prophet kept
before his audience the missionary vocation to which God had called
Israel. In order to do that, he began by producing a monograph dealing
with the kind of God who had brought Israel into captivity and was
about to redeem her!

I. A God Who Forgives (40:1-2)

There is no greater consolation than the knowledge that our sins have
been dealt with, and we are free from their penalty! Nothing motivates
for effective service more than the certainty that the record is clear of
guilt from our past transgressions! What can even begin to compare with
the statement of our Savior to the defeated woman, "Neither do I condemn thee: go thy way; from henceforth sin no more" (John 8:11). This
first poem, best understood as a prologue to the entire larger section,
announces good news, employing a form of dialogue which recurs
throughout the subsequent material. Sometimes we find it difficult to
distinguish the speakers, but in this opening statement, no doubt exists
concerning the identification. God Himself shouts to the prophet His
own format for introducing the message. Speak to Israel's heart! They
are a people whose sins have been removed from God's presence!

Old Testament Grace

A word of caution at this point! This was not the "salvation by grace"
set forth so clearly for the individual in the New Testament, especially
by the apostle Paul. The prophet was dealing with national Israel. She
had paid her debt. The literal Hebrew reads, "Her military service has
been fulfilled, her guilt has been paid off." Only in the expression, "hath

received . . . double for all her sins" do we find any variation from the divine law of sin and retribution, and this is probably an Oriental figure of speech or, as someone has called it, "not the language of mathematics but the language of grace." The God of holiness is also One who is rich in mercy and compassionate understanding. He is ready to receive Israel again for service in His redemptive program.

The Chosen Must Obey

Why was the nation called upon to endure such hardships? The answer is self-evident. Israel was a chosen vessel and must be taught that neither an individual nor a nation can sin with impunity. God told Ananias that Saul was "a chosen vessel unto me, to bear my name before the Gentiles" and said "I will show him how many things he must suffer for my name's sake" (Acts 9:15-16). The parallel is not exact, but the basic principle is the same. Paul, in his pre-Christian days, intensely amplified persecution against the Christians. After his conversion he suffered the thorns from the tree he planted, leaving us a lesson that the "historical reality factor" in life is real even after one becomes a Christian. Israel had been chosen by God to reveal and implement His redemptive program, but she still had to suffer when she sinned. Those who serve God in special ways must also play by the rules.

Still, however, grace shines through the words of the prophet. No one can truly secure freedom from the wages of sin by enduring the punishment due. Sin is too terrible! If God had not held back His chastening even punitive hand, Israel would have been destroyed—no more than she deserved. One prominent scholar suggests the "double for all her sins" is a phrase borrowed from the ancient custom of a benefactor folding the parchment on which a person's debts were outlined, marking it paid, and sealing it to the door of the creditors, indicating that man had received double for all his indebtedness. While, to some, this analogy is suspect, surely some contemporary figure of speech must have been utilized by the prophet since we can never think of God as being unfair in punishing sin. Perhaps this was the heart of a compassionate God crying out in anguish, perhaps overstating the case for effect, and actually issuing an early pardon because He felt Israel had received sufficient discipline for her iniquities. Whatever the meaning, the nation was now ready once more to resume her role as God's present messiah to bring the true Messiah into the world!

II. A God Who Demonstrates His Glory (40:3-5)

Who was the crying voice? This figure of speech is an allusion to the practice of Eastern monarchs who, when embarking on a journey through a barren, unfrequented, or inhospitable country, sent heralds before to prepare the way. Since such expeditions often involved the necessity of marching through places that had no public highways for movement of troops, someone had to provide supplies, make bridges, ford streams, level hills, construct causeways over valleys or fill them up, and make a way through any forest that might lie in the intended line of march. The prophet heard a noise resembling a long trumpet blast but actually was the "outrider" of the king, the one that went before and announced his coming.

Glory of Israel's God

Rather than a mere solitary voice, the prophet must have heard the whole heavens ringing with shouts and commands as God's generals prepared the way for the King of kings. His language soared as he spoke of God's majesty and dominion. Earlier writers used the word *glory* to describe the visible manifestation of God, the One who to them was essentially invisible and incomprehensible. Originally, the Old Testament declared that no one could see God and live. Later, however, religious leaders used the term in a different way, regarding God's glory as the visible medium through which His presence revealed itself to humans.

To the devotees of Canaanite religion, light and fire were used to denote the radiating power of a deity. Israel took over this concept and purified it. At first, she felt the glory was an actual revelation of God's invisible heart. In earlier days it was easy to confuse the idea of glory, pictured as fire, with various meteorological phenomena such as lightning or volcanic eruptions. The prophets, however, refined and injected moral content into the concept. In this context, however, the ultimate meaning of the word is reached. The seed is sown that would later blossom forth as redemptive, recreative, and suffering love. God's greatest glory is His atoning sacrifice for a sinful world! As the old hymn says: "Down at the cross where my Saviour died, . . . Glory to his name"!

The herald was a roadmaker, the hastener of a better and holier day. Several things were necessary to perform such a function: a profound sense of the evil present in his day; an unquenchable faith in the future; and readiness to serve and to suffer if necessary.

Righteousness Must Reign

Where God's glory appears, people see divine sovereignty not merely as a future possibility but as the present reality on which everything in life depends. When God truly reigns in human affairs, two phenomena take place. Not only do the righteous rejoice, but the unrighteous tremble. The fundamental blindness of which humankind stands guilty is an unawareness of the fundamental basis by which this universe holds together: the rule of God. The world is constituted in such a way that righteousness not only will reign, but it must reign because the God of holiness is sovereign.

> I know that right is right;
> That it is not good to lie;
> That love is better than spite;
> And a neighbor than a spy.
>
> I know that passions need
> The leash of a sober mind;
> I know that each good deed
> Some sure reward will find.
>
> In the darkest night of the year
> When the stars are all gone out
> That courage is better than fear
> That faith is truer than doubt.
>
> And fierce though the fiends may fight
> And long though the sun may hide
> I know that truth and right
> Have the universe on their side.
> —Washington Gladden

God's reflected holiness is His glory. In the inaugural vision which ushered him into his calling, Isaiah heard the seraphim speak three times of God's holiness before they spoke of His glory. J. A. Alexander said it beautifully, "To see God's glory is a common expression for recognizing his presence and agency in any event." The difference in the glory to be revealed in the Babylonian Exodus as contrasted with the previous one is that in the coming out of Egypt, God revealed His glory to Israel and, in a sense, to the country from which He delivered her, but now He will manifest his power and holiness to the entire world—"all flesh shall see it together" (v. 5). To limit these words to a restoration of the Jews is not only gratuitous but inconsistent with the strength and comprehensiveness of its expressions. The glory of God will be universally displayed. This promise is far too extensive to be fully verified in an isolated event or period of history. The Gentiles are not "second-class citizens" in God's kingdom nor an afterthought in His redemptive plan. He had them in mind from the beginning. God so loved the world, all of it, that He gave His Son!

III. A God Whose Word Endures (40:6-8)

How can such wonderful promises be realized in the face of pagan pomp and power? Once again, the prophet heard a voice. The immediate purpose of it was to reassure the exiles that, though they were surrounded by the imposing fabric of a great empire, crushed into silent submission by its power, and awed by its splendor, God had not forgotten them. Many scholars, feeling the traditional translation "cry" is colorless and misleading, render the command to the prophet as "preach." The voice came directly to him, and he answered personally. The Qumran text verifies this, reading, "And I said, what shall I preach?" We do not have the prophet overhearing a conversation between heavenly beings but rather a direct revelation from God. He did not have the full message, but he was no longer in a state of uncertainty with no good news to proclaim. He knew enough to proclaim distinctly that, while everything else was fading and transitory, God's promise was firm and secure.

Disobedience Brings Judgment

If one sees a beautiful hillside covered with spring flowers and returns a few weeks later to discover that not one of those flowers survived, one understands the stark reality with which the prophet approached the matter of human life and its brevity. Israel's history paralleled this truth. When she obeyed God's Word, her national life contained vitality and fulfillment, but stubborn resistance to the divine standards brought her into a condition that resembled violent death! As God's breath, the wind, blows upon the grass and makes it wither, so one who violates the moral and spiritual laws by which the world is constituted reaps the wind of judgment and the whirlwind of devastation.

Only God's Word endures! Humankind's ultimate hope is in recognizing that, of ourselves and by ourselves, we are nothing. God's breath that created us can wither us, just as the hot wind from the desert withered the sparse grass of the dry Babylonian sand dunes, leaving them without beauty, energy, health, or wisdom. Constant, reliable, steadfast, and alive forevermore, God's Word stands eternally because it has issued from the very heart of Him who is holiness and mercy combined. Such a mingling of attributes always outlives everything and everyone who oppose it. Permanent character is perhaps the best description of God's Word. In contrast to the weak, transitory nature of all things associated with human flesh, God's Word which reflects His eternal truth cannot be annulled or changed.

New Testament Brings Final Truth

In the New Testament, two allusions to this passage, or at least the truth of it, give further insight into its deeper meaning. Simon Peter spoke of the Christian as one who has been born again "not of corruptible seed, but of incorruptible, through the Word of God, which liveth and abideth" (1 Pet. 1:23). He then quoted the Old Testament prophet's words concerning flesh and grass, the fact that they fail, but God's Word abides forever. His final words relate this to the gospel which had been preached to them. Peter's conclusion is crystal clear. God's Word is the good news about Jesus. In the prophet, the truth is in embryo, hidden within the mystery of national Israel. In Jesus, however, that which was implicit has become indisputably explicit. The gospel is God's final word to humankind. In the prologue to John's Gospel, this truth reaches its ultimate fulfillment. The "Word" which was in the beginning with God and by whom God made the world has become flesh in Jesus Christ. In the Eternal Word that became man, we see the glory of God in its fullest form. This truth is eternal and shall never pass away.

Importance of Written Word

In a larger sense, the Word of God means every word that proceedeth from the Heavenly Father. But in a practical and restricted sense, it is our present-day Bible. We do not need to argue whether our Bible *contains* the Word of God or *is* the Word of God. *Both are true!* Collectively, the sixty-six canonized books contain the revealed message, progressively given as the people were able to receive it. Existentially, not every word within the sacred library is a direct quote from the first member of the Trinity for we have words of Eliphaz, Bildad, Zophar, Ahaz, Pharaoh, Jezebel, Sanballat, Tobiah, Geshem, the wild and rambling words of Job, and even quotes from the devil himself. Yet, for all practical purposes, we are not incorrect when we refer to our present-day Bible as the Word of God. The totality of it is God's message to us.

The Bible lives! Why does it live? Samuel Taylor Coleridge said, "it found him" and it "finds us" also. It finds us when we sin and holds up to us the offer of forgiveness. It finds us when we wonder about God, and it reveals God to us, calling us back to faith in Him. It finds us when we need inspiration for the rough spots in life. We do not need to defend it in the marketplace. The Bible can take care of itself if only we will proclaim it and live by its teachings!

IV. A God Who Both Conquers and Shepherds (40:9-11)

Assyrian and Babylonian sculptures, discovered by archaeologists, reveal how captives were treated in ancient days. Driven in gangs, they were pushed on by soldiers in the ranks while the weak who could not keep pace were tossed aside to die. Experiences like these must have burned into the memory of a nation. What joy the prophet's words must have brought that their Lord would not permit them to be slaves forever in a foreign land! The verb *tellest good news* comes from a root that means to "smooth out the wrinkles on a human face." The city of Jerusalem had lain in ruins for nearly two generations, but the sad and desolate widow could now rejoice, for her day of redemption was rapidly approaching. Scholars vary as to whether the messenger was the prophet himself or the city Jerusalem, also called Zion, that is commanded to speak from the mountaintop the good news to the peasants in the vicinity who had lived in poverty during the time Israel had been captive in Babylon. The point, however, is not who spoke but what was said. The remnant in Babylon had been told that God's Word remains forever and that a spiritual nucleus now must pass the message to the poverty stricken back home.

A New Joy

Upon hearing the good news, those careworn and desolate villagers would experience a joy they had not known for many years. Despite all appearances to the contrary, their covenant God still lived. Such an announcement called for a public gathering to rejoice in victory, with females assembling as in days of old to celebrate the tidings with songs, dances, and rejoicings. The "be not afraid" refers not to fear of telling the news so much as the assurance that one does not have to be concerned about being contradicted by an enemy or embarassed at the promise not being fulfilled. The prophet had already stated that "all flesh shall see it," and thus there should be no doubt about a divine pronouncement. Do not be afraid! God lives! Because of this, His decrees will never fail!

Power and Mercy

The God of Israel is twofold! The prophet combined the image of a conquering king with that of a gentle shepherd. Actually, the two were not as far apart in the ancient mind as they are to us today. Ancient Eastern kings often adopted the title "shepherd of his people." This indicated that human sovereignty called for two qualities: strength to maintain order against divisive forces from within and enemy attacks from without, and the gentleness of a shepherd who watches over his flock. Likewise, God, to establish His rule among people, must be tough yet tender to meet the needs of His people.

Israel needed a God of power! When we understand the background of that day, we realize their complaint was that events which determined destiny seem to have been without plan or direction. They felt God had abdicated His place of authority, and the world was like a driverless car headed for a ditch. Israel also, however, needed a God of compassion! Long before Jesus saw the multitude as "sheep not having a shepherd" (Matt. 9:36), Israel felt that way about herself. For centuries she had been kicked up and down the field of international politics. The final blow came upon Jerusalem in 586 BC, after an eighteen-month siege. A few were present in Babylon who remembered that tragic event. Others had heard about it so many times they felt they had actually seen it. In the homeland, sheep without a shepherd were helpless to defend themselves against enemies. Perhaps no more appropriate figure of speech could have been chosen by the prophet. The people could identify with the similarity to their own predicament, and no better news could have come than that they had an unseen Shepherd who understood their problem and, better still, would minister pastorally to them. The moment had arrived for an approach of comfort. God had used the Exile with all its sorrows and trials to reveal His nature as primarily saving love.

In every generation, humans need the twofold function of God. No weak God can deal with sin. He must be, first of all, a conquering hero who defeats satanic forces and wins the victory over entrenched evil. Behind the infinitudes of space and the inexorableness of law, human beings also need a tenderness that consoles. We, like sheep, are creatures without judgment or foresight and must be guarded against our own folly. Human love is not blind in spite of that persistent cliche. No husband or wife is blind to their companion's faults. The thrill is that we love our spouses in spite of shortcomings. God's love is greater! God demonstrated His love for us in that while we were sinners, Christ died for us.

Hold both these truths in mind! God's love must never be thought of as caprice. Divine grace is as infinitely strong as the procession of stars. Mountains may depart, and hills may be removed, but God's love will not depart from His own. God's kindness is the inner side of His strength. We need both sides of God, and, praise His name, both are present and available for us in Jesus Christ!

V. A God Who Is Resourceful (40:12-17)

The prophet followed his panoramic picture of God's greatness with three simple but profound illustrations—the magnitude of His operations as Creator, the perfection and sufficiency of His knowledge, and the insignificance in comparison with Him of all that exists. The questions set forth are rhetorical, not demanding an answer. The only reply that could come forth is that God alone is capable of measuring, meting, and weighing such huge masses of the material world, giving to them suitable shapes, forms, and proportions.

The Creator Rules

Of course, the prophet spoke against the background of the people's concept of a "three-decker universe" which was the generally accepted view as a scientific description of the cosmos they knew. Although the Jews had, for centuries, feared the sea and had little to do with it, refusing to venture out upon it unless absolute necessary, they dreaded even more the waters of chaos under the earth, considering them as symbolic of all that was evil and inchoate. When the prophet spoke of God as comprehending the dust of the earth "in a measure" which means literally "with a third," he may have been speaking against the background of a traditional ancient interpretation that the world was divided into three parts—one-third wilderness, one-third habitable land, and one-third seas and rivers. Whatever the nuances of the phrases used, the main thrust is that the God who "started the whole thing" keeps both His eye and hand on it. Pluralistic cultures may have had their spiritually inferior and often morally disgusting "creation" stories, but the Jewish mind held tenaciously to a personal Creator who brought the world into existence and continues to monitor its activity. The Hebrews called the first cause "God," and no one possessed His resources or even came a "close second." No cramping limitations could His majesty express! Supreme in power and holiness and glorious in His grace!

God is Wise

The cosmological argument for God is good, but the teleological one is better. The universe shows design because a mastermind planned it. Not only "intelligence" but, even more important, "spirit" brought it into being, for this is the literal meaning of the word rendered *mind* in most traditional versions. The One who needed no assistance in his architectural or engineering plans as he "stretched out the heavens as a tent to dwell in" likewise needed no aid in moral and ethical matters. He possesses keen discernment and uncanny insight into human motives. Not only is God the Eternal Word, but also He is Infinite Wisdom. The struggling patriarch pointed out that wisdom "is not to be found among men" and then testified, "God alone . . . Knows the place where wisdom is found, because he sees the ends of the earth, Sees everything under the sky" (Job 28:13,23, GNB). Paul, of course, brought the concept to its highest fulfillment when he spoke of Christ as the power of God and the wisdom of God (1 Cor. 1:24). Unfailing Source of guidance! Unending Fount of lore! O what a royal privilege, such wisdom to explore!

The Lord Is Above All

Although we live today in a vastly more expansive universe than the prophet could ever have imagined, his similes resound as vibrantly and validly for us as they could possibly have to the exiles preparing to return home. Think of a bucket being drawn up from a well. A drop or two spills back, but they are not worth catching in comparison with that left in the bucket. So God regards the nations when compared to His infinite resources. Again, visualize small particles of dust. God regards the nations in this light. This particular figure of speech is even more enhanced for us since we are extremely conscious of living in a world that is an "agglomeration of infinitely tiny atoms." Closely related to the previous picture, the prophet considered the isles in the Mediterranean, probably a symbol for all nations, as small particles lifted up and blown away. All three comparisons emphasize the comparative nothingness of the material world in the presence of Israel's God who rules over the destinies of all humankind.

Changing the area of emphasis, the prophet turned to the religious sector. Humanity, instinctively religious, has always sought a proper sacrifice as homage to the god it serves. Look at Lebanon, the mountainous area to the north where the beautiful cedars grew, immortalized by Solomon who used them as interior decoration for the Temple. Neither her mighty forests nor her abundance of animals could properly supply an altar to the God who was about to deliver his people from Babylonian bondage. Not only is Israel's God One who outruns all the calculations of humankind and so resourceful He cannot be "crammed into a human cranium," but He towers above the religious concepts of the nations whom He considers as nonentities.

VI. A God Who Is Incomparable (40:18-26)

What is God like? With what words do we describe Him? Because we are human, we have no option but to speak of Him in terms of our existence and characteristics. Scholars use the term *anthropomorphic* concerning many biblical pictures of God, a word brought into being by a combination of two Greek words which mean "man" and "form." With our limited insights and lack of ability to communicate, we often think of God as only related to our qualities. Thus, we speak of God's hand, heart, feet, as well as His laughter, anger, memory, and purpose. If we wish, however, to know God in His fullness, we must experience Him as a spiritual being. To meet God "face-to-face" means literally to enter into deep personal fellowship with Him in such a way that we know His will as surely as if He spoke to us with an audible voice.

Idolatry—Then and Now

Idolatry has always been a subtle thing. It is so sophisticated in our day we often do not recognize its silent nuances. We have come a long way from the crude practices of the Babylonians and the others, but the basic principle is the same. They constructed a material god to a concept and then worshiped it, following the formal ritual with a practice of the idea personified. We do the indulging without bothering to make the idol and give token allegiance to it. The prophet spoke sarcastically of the graven images, some overlaid with gold or silver and some only made of wood. These human efforts to conceive of and reproduce God in tangible form fell far short of the truly divine Person that they were not only crude but downright insulting to the One who "sitteth above the circle of the earth" and to whom the inhabitants are as "grasshoppers" (40:22). Israel's God, she needed to know and never forget, was One in whose hands the destiny of kings and governors as well as civil and military leaders was held. Though scarcely planted and sown so their stock could take root, God's breath blew on them, and they were dispersed as chaff! So "wholly other" is God that human efforts to conceive of Him in any way borders on blasphemy, especially when all we can produce is a fatuous gold-lacquered image which must be chained to a wall, so it will remain upright.

The prophet hurled the challenge again, putting words into the mouth of God Himself, "To whom then will ye liken me, that I should be equal?" (40:25), bringing the visible structure of the universe before the people to express the majesty and wonder of the Creator over against the sinfulness and pettiness of the creature. Since God's cosmological masterpiece outlives individual nations and empires, humanity placed against the backdrop of the universe becomes utterly insignificant. How dare we even begin to make ourselves or anything else on a peer level with God!

The Prophet's Challenge

Look up! What do you see! Stars, the heavenly host! God knows them all by name! The prophet's words remind us of Napoleon's famous reply to the atheistic group. He pointed to the skies and said, "No God? But, gentlemen, who made these?" Whether or not the Israelites had been influenced by Babylonian ideas and were confusing their God with astral deities can never be ascertained nor is it important in understanding the

prophet's words. A hardheaded, hard-driving man, not noted for spiritu-
ality, said once that the most religious experience he had ever known was
in a planetarium where, before his eyes, was unrolled the spectacle of the
universe in its unity, order, simplicity, and intelligibility. "Man," he said,
"chance doesn't fit in. There is mind in that." Joseph Addison put it
beautifully and irrefutably:

> In reason's ear, they all rejoice
> And utter forth a glorious voice
> Forever singing as they shine
> The hand that made us is divine.

Though the world in which the Israelites lived was dark night, chaotic,
and disoriented, and they mingled with captives from many lands in the
midst of confused tongues and alien customs, as well as diverse religious
beliefs, even the most discouraged could see God if they would only look
up and behold the Lord's starry host!

VII. A God Who Enables (40:27-31)

Concluding his masterful monograph on God's greatness, the prophet
turned to the people with a personal word. In light of all God had done
for them in years past, how could they feel He was either unobservant
of their fate or indifferent to it? In fairness to the exiles, we must, of
course, recognize the years of banishment and humiliation had continued
far beyond that which might seem reasonable to any person. Since the
cry of despondency is human, a sense of insignificance or prolonged
suffering can cause it to come upon us quickly and severely. If we feel
God delays His answer to our prayers or ignores them, or if a friend
disappoints us, we often cry until our lips are white with pain that we
have been forsaken.

The poetic parallelism with which the prophet addressed the people,
however, calling them Jacob and Israel, should have brought historical
associations to their mind. Once more, he shouted, "Have ye not known,
have ye not heard" (40:21,28)? The remarkable accumulation of titles for
Israel's Deity shows the prophet was moving first through what one
called a "dizzy pinnacle" but then to a spiritual climax. Though God has
been around a long time, He is "amazingly young for His age."

God's Resources Needed

The apostle Paul centuries later also recognized the need for God's presence to make him superior to circumstances. He found that power, of course, in the living Christ who was the highest form of revelation ever made to mankind. Israel in her day, however, had sufficient knowledge of God to give encouragement and vitality for coping with the problems brought about by disenchantment and frustration. A proper awareness of God's resources can produce an inflow of divine strength that will redirect you toward a victorious approach to life. Decay of energy and loss of enthusiasm comes to all of us at times, but a personal fellowship with God can make even the weakest person strong.

God gives His strength in graduated steps according to each one's need. All human strength will eventually deteriorate and grow weak. Alexander Maclaren pointed out that in our early days we dream of life as a "kind of enchanted garden, full of all manner of delights." We stand at the threshold with eager eyes and outstretched hands. Long before we have gone very far, we often become sick and tired of the whole thing and weary of what is laid upon us. God gives strength and divine energy for every stage of the journey.

Faithfulness Is Required

Soaring requires that we have wings—elevation, vision, buoyancy. Running means we must have capacity to meet the stress and strain of trying times. Walking demands the most resources to meet the humdrum dullness of ordinary days with their frustrations and irritations. We must keep on the regular rounds, both steadily and saintly, even when the sky is gray, and the way is monotonous. This may sound like the reversal of priorities, a sort of working up to an anticlimax, but the opposite is true! Walking, in the Christian life, is much more difficult than flying. Perhaps the greatest demonstration of God's traits is that He can perpetually reinforce us from within, suiting a graduated ability according to our needs.

Patience Is Essential

How is this goal achieved? The prophet said that they who wait upon the Lord "shall renew their strength" (v. 31). Perhaps the most essential ingredient of faith is the willingness to have sufficient patience to wait until God acts in our behalf or gives us the strength to do it for ourselves. Whatever else faith is, it rings with optimism and relaxes with certainty.

As the symphonic prophecy progresses, the themes will grow in number, and each will gain intensity. The initial thrust, however, has gone forth. Above everything else, God comforts! No matter how dark the sky, discouraging the circumstances, or desperate the situation, we can depend on God. Because He is merciful, He never forgets, and because He is all powerful, He never fails. God rules, redeems, and reinforces. Great is the Lord and greatly to be praised!

2
Two Coins in the Fountain
(41:1-29)

Whether we view the prophetic oracles in this general section as one continuous sermon spoken on a specific occasion or regard them as a series of isolated poems, one thing is certain. The chapters, as they appear in the text, interlock beautifully, and each one artistically introduces a new feature. As is true in all symphonic renditions, a number of themes revolve around a major one. Each is introduced, expanded, and then dropped, but the main thrust goes on, gaining intensity as the masterpiece develops.

Redemption or deliverance, the major Old Testament concept of salvation, dominates the final twenty-seven chapters of this great prophetic book. One scholar gives a simple but provocative analysis, dividing the chapters into Deliverance (40—48), Deliverer (49—57), and Delivered (58—66). Some of the lesser motifs appearing earlier but then blending into the overall work are: the sovereignty of Israel's God; the folly of idolatry; the appeal to predictive prophecy; the servanthood of Israel; the place of Cyrus the Great in God's purpose; and the prediction of Babylon's fall as a prelude to the liberation and restoration of the Jews.

Although interpreters vary, one of the most popular approaches is to see this segment before us as similar to the great arraignment (1:1-31), a prophetic drama presented as a courtroom scene. The material deals with the absolute sovereignty and sole deity of Israel's omnipotent God as one side of the coin and the utter folly of idol worship as the other. Someone has said graphically that we have "two coins in the fountain" of God's justice. One coin testifies to God's unequaled power, and the other coin points out the helplessness of anything or anyone that seeks to usurp His position as our Redeemer and Provider. Three clearly recognized sections open up which enable us to examine the prophet's words with clarity and profit. First, A Word of Confrontation to the

Nations (41:1-7). Second, A Word of Comfort for Israel (41:8-20). Third, A Word of Challenge to the Idols (41:21-29).

I. Confrontation (41:1-7)

Although the term *islands* referred specifically to the small bodies of land in the Mediterranean Sea, it often stood for "distant lands" and, in some cases, all the existing nations of the world as Israel knew it. Like the foreign prophecies of the canonical prophets, we have the problem of whether the messenger spoke these words directly to the nations or used this unusual and graphic literary device to send an unforgettable message to Israel. The latter seems most likely, but we should not rule out the former. After all, Jonah made a "missionary trip" to Assyria and, as some one has jokingly said, he was only one of the "minor prophets."

Voicing His message through His chosen spokesman, the Lord of history called the nations to a court of law as He, the Sovereign of the universe, has the right to do. He commanded them to forget their military exploits and realize that He alone has power over the affairs of nations. Before they said any word in defense of their position, they were to find their strength in the true God who empowers both the strong and the weak. Although only the first of the four verbs in verse 1 is an imperative, the other three, which are imperfects, retain the force of the first command. The prophet spoke with authority because his words came directly from God.

Cyrus the Conquerer

Look at the one whom Israel's God had brought on the scene! Only Cyrus the Great fits the picture although a few scholars still hold out for Abraham who defeated the four kings of the East (Gen. 14:1-16) and rescued Lot. This man's military career was amazing. No one but God could have given him such instant success. Only the king of a small country when he began, Cyrus annexed Media to Elam, laying the foundation for a great empire which would control the destinies of Western Asia for more than two-hundred years. He overthrew Croesus, the wealthy king of Lydia, whose capital, Sardis, with its fabulous treasures, fell into his hands in 540 BC. The crowning enterprise of his military career was when he incorporated Babylon into his expanding Medo-Persian Empire. Two differing stories tell of the city's fall, both probably having an element of truth in them. First, Cyrus diverted the course of the Euphrates and came into the city through the riverbed without any loss of men. Second, the people were so disgusted with their rulers that they opened the doors of the city from the inside and welcomed the liberator, preferring him to the excessive oppression and luxurious indulgences of their own leaders.

The prophet used the word *righteousness* to describe the Lord's projecting Cyrus into the fray. Although the word's meaning may be "deliverance, victory, or even prosperity," the prophet's thrust, certainly his primary one, is that God placed His anointing hand on Cyrus in order to use him, nonbeliever though he was, to bring about another step in the divine plan for world redemption. The Israelites had served their sentence, and God was ready to bring them home. Babylon was too sin soaked and idolatry oriented to give a decree for the captives to be released. God raised up an outsider and "girded" him for the task though Cyrus did not know the role he was performing.

A Divine Paradox

A great lesson emerges for us at this point that needs to be repeated often. God can, and often does, use nongodly, sometimes even terribly wicked people, to accomplish His purposes in this world, especially in directing the affairs of His own people. Although Isaiah's preaching could not do it, Sennacherib brought Jerusalem to her knees, and the city was spared for a century. When evangelicals refuse to accept the full implications of the gospel, God often raises up some who are outside the institutional church to "stir up the waters" and force the people of "orthodox" Christianity to accept their obligations. If "born-again believers" refuse to accept God's will in their personal lives, an arrogant, overbearing, even wicked person can so arrange affairs that tney are required to do it because of extenuating circumstances. Ironic though it may be, some of the great humanitarian movements in history have been brought about by those who had no formal identification with organized religion.

Prophetic Irony

A common enemy causes the natural human reaction of making people forget old quarrels and encourage each other as they resist the conquerer. The prophet presented a "cameo" to show how people will "whistle in the dark" to keep up their courage. As the crisis developed because of the conquerer's triumphs, the politicians, merchants, crafts-men, and people rushed to a mutual-assistance pact. The religious hierar-chy and the "god makers" overhauled old deities and created new ones. They felt adequate pantheon was essential for the critical hour: With biting irony, the prophet gave a brief glimpse into the idol manufacturing business. Those scholars who seek to rearrange the text and transfer this description (41:6-7) to another context (40:20) fail to understand the prophet was bringing both sides of the coin in this one part of his message. Only Israel's God is supreme and worthy of human allegiance! Idol worship is idle worship!

Modern Idolatry

A practical word needs to be said about idolatry in our day. A false *mental* image of God is just as dangerous to spiritual worship as a false *metal* image. We are bathed constantly in the aura of materialism, the "golden calf" of our day. Religion is not the "opiate of the people." Not now! A luxurious life-style combined with commercialized entertain-ment dulls and tranquilizes the senses of modern people! Covetousness, which Paul called idolatry, eats its way into our character, and, before we realize it, we are bowing to our idols of greed and compromising every principle we ever held in order to obtain a false security which we mistake for the real thing. Too often, our days are filled only with tangibles. God has become merely an ever-present help in time of trouble (Ps.46:1). A wise Christian layperson said, "The divine glow of the Christian life does not go out suddenly: it just fades out because we cannot touch, see, taste, hear, and smell the Lord's presence." How can we become less material and more spiritually minded? There is one way! Batten down the door of selfishness, and we will find the transition from our own boots to the other fellow's shoes can be a delight. A golden calf, like a lovely lamp, can easily lose its luster, causing us to strive for new and more glamorous ones, but those who are constrained by the love of Christ will find their desire for such things diminishing and, hopefully, at last disappearing. G. Campbell Morgan was certainly correct when he said that idolatry results from the loss of the vision of God, and, though God's love is eternal, it is never divorced from moral requirements. He asked and answered, "If we are guilty of idolatry, what will cure us? The vision of Him, as He was seen in Jesus Christ."

II. Comfort (41:8-20)

The scene changes! A superficial reading might suggest a digression took place as the prophet switched from Cyrus the conquerer, unconsciously executing God's will and implementing the divine program to Israel, God's servant, weak though she is at present. Beneath the apparent disconnectedness, however, closer study shows a real continuity of thought in the entire material. The courtroom scene opens with a discussion between God and the nations (41:1-7) and closes with one between God and the heathen idols.

These ideal representations, however, have no reality apart from the part they take in concrete form as historical events unfold. God's controversy with the nations is based on His providence, especially in vindicating the "right" of Israel against the world. The opposition Israel suffered from the heathen resulted from the antagonism between true spiritual religion and blind, crude, immoral idolatry. The essential identity of interest between God and His people forms the basis for the prophet's introduction of Israel in her proposed function as the organ of the Lord's redemptive purpose in history. Israel had no need to fear the advance of Cyrus because he was God's chosen instrument to overthrow idolatrous Babylon, and his victory would guarantee the restoration of Israel to her homeland where she would once more be in God's will, serving as the channel through whom the Messiah would eventually come.

The True Israel

Four distinct truths can be traced in God's words to Israel. First, because she possessed a unique relation to the Lord (41:8-10), she should not fear. How odd of God, to choose the Jews! Not Egypt with centuries of civilization behind her! Not Assyria, strong in military might! Not Greece with her linguistic and cultural longevity! Not Rome with her organizational genius! Rather, He chose a slave people in a foreign land whose father had been a wandering Aramean, ready to perish (Deut. 26:5), and made them the recipient of His highest revelation. His sixfold promise to Abraham (Gen. 12:1-3) stands unequaled in history, but we need to remember the main thrust of God's words, His reason for blessing the patriarch's descendants. They were to be a blessing! In and through them, all the nations of the world would be blessed.

Israel was a servant to be used, not a king to be glorified or a superrace to enjoy certain privileges because of origin. She was to be a kingdom of priests that would lead the people to God, not a god to whom the people should come. Though, in a limited sense, national Israel was, in that day, the "seed of Abraham," Paul made it clear that the true seed of Abraham is not physical Israel but the spiritual family that receives Jesus Christ as Savior and Lord (Gal. 3:29). Nothing can be plainer than the words of the apostle who said, "Now to Abraham were the promises spoken, and to his seed. He saith not, And to seeds, as of many; but as of one. And to thy seed, which is Christ" (Gal. 3:16). This truth needs to be nailed down before one goes any further in considering Israel's relationship to God.

Friendship, Love, and Service

The group about to return home, however, was, at that present moment, God's servant with a clearly defined mission though they were not fully cognizant of all the implications within their task. Some scholars contend the phrases "taken hold of from the ends of the earth" and "called from the corners thereof" (v. 9) refer to Abraham who came from Ur to Canaan while others suggest a number of other Israelites came at the same general time period, the close of the Babylonian captivity, to Judah for the purpose of joining their fellow countrymen in rebuilding the city. One possible interpretation is that since, to the Jew, Jerusalem was the "navel" of the earth, Mesopotamia, from where Abraham came, and Egypt, from which the slaves were delivered, constituted the two extremes or the "ends" of the earth, but this is a forced exegesis if it can be called that at all.

God called Abraham His "friend" because, as one Hebrew scholar notes, the language has no word that expresses the reciprocal relationship of friendship as distinct from companionship. This fact, no doubt, influenced the thinking of such prophets as Hosea and Jeremiah who presented the concept of Israel as the bride or wife of her God. Archaeologists have discovered jars and seals with the words "Servant of the king" stamped on them, indicating this was probably a technical term for a royal official. Israel thus knew what she was meant to be as God's servant, one who served unquestionably and eagerly, always ready to execute the will of her royal Master.

Love echoes through the pages of both the Old and New Testaments but nowhere any more beautifully than when God says to weak, fearful Israel, who in the depths of despair cringes in anticipation of what her enemies can do, "I have chosen thee and have not cast thee away" (41:9), then quickly adding, "I will strengthen thee; . . . help thee; . . . uphold thee with the right hand of my righteousness" (41:10). The "be not dismayed" which is sandwiched between the two assurances means literally, "do not gaze about in anxiety." "Fear not" or its equivalent occurs often in the Bible. In no context, however, is it more meaningful than in the promises made to those who are in the process of serving as God's chosen vessel to bring about His redemptive program for the world. To Abraham (Gen. 15:1), Isaac (Gen. 26:24), and Jacob (Gen. 46:3), God gave assurance with this phrase that the messianic plan would be consumated in spite of difficulties. To Israel, during the Babylonian captivity, the promise was repeated. God's plans may be delayed because of human sin, but they will not be defeated.

Whatever firmness or stability Israel needed in order to meet the future events of her national life, God would provide. The basis of His empowering action, however, is an ethical one. He will uphold her "with the right hand of . . . righteousness" (41:10). To Israel, He will exhibit this righteousness with a blessing, but, to the nations who do not know God and oppose His work, it will appear in the punitive and retributive justice meted out for their wickedness.

God Will Protect

The second distinct truth trumpeted by the prophet was that, humanly speaking, Israel might have cause to fear since she was surrounded by enemies, but she must not forget that God can and would put them to utter confusion (41:11-13). Israel needed to remember that those who were fighting against her were fighting against God's purposes in her. This does not mean that Israel was always right! Far from it! She was, however, always Israel, the people God had anointed to implement His plan for worldwide redemption.

A trilogy of phrases, with an inserted statement between the second and third saying that those who contended against Israel would disappear, presents a graphic literary style. The results are stated first and then a description of the activities carried on by Israel's enemies, emphasizing what was not done by the fruit of the deeds. A literal translation reads, "They shall be ashamed and humiliated, those who are incensed against thee. They shall become as nothing and shall perish, those who took thee to court. They shall become as nothing at all, those who have been warring against thee" (vv. 11-12). Some scholars contend the phrase "incensed against thee" translates another verb and reads, "who snort with indignation against thee," but one must change the vowel pointing of the Hebrew text to get this translation, and no evidence can be found to warrant such a change. We should let the Masoretic scholars insert the vowels. After all, they were much closer to the language! Either translation, however, is equally graphic and, no doubt, an accurate image of the prophet's inner feelings as he spoke.

Although the prophet's words were general, and we should show caution in seeking to find a particular application for such words, one fact stands out as true which would give credence to the message. None of the people whom historical Israel had known as neighbors, whether friendly or hostile, survived into the middle of the sixth century except Babylon, and her fate was already discernible in the figure of Cyrus. If all Israel's past had vanished, why should she fear? Only divine judgment could annihilate her, and God had already promised that she had suffered sufficiently for her sins. He planned to use her to accomplish his redemptive work and, therefore, she was held securely in the reliable, rocklike right hand of God's righteousness. The contrasts which the prophet employed made the truth stand out more clearly. God would sustain Israel but all of her enemies would be completely destroyed. What other assurance could Israel possibly need or want!

Elimination of Adversaries

As the same theme continued, the prophet added a third truth to his message, declaring that Israel herself, with the Lord's aid, would be the means of crushing and scattering the foes which threatened both her present and future security (41:14-16). Since Israel was neither rich nor populous, she was powerless. The term *worm* symbolized meekness and humility rather than moral depravity. An insect crawling upon the ground stands in jeopardy as it is at the mercy of every person who passes by. The term *men of Israel* means literally "dead ones," an apt description of the people in Exile. The redeemer in Israel's domestic life was the nearest male relative whose duty it was to redeem or buy back a person who had sold himself or his property if he were killed that the widow receive the family estate. He also avenged the blood of one who was murdered. The term had a warm place in Israel's social and religious life and combined with the "Holy One" concept of God joined the two essential elements of Hebrew religion as revealed through the Law and the Prophets. God is one who insists on righteousness, but He is rich in mercy to those who fall short of His standard.

The figure which the prophet used as a practical demonstration of how Israel would implement God's redemptive program must have aroused heightened interest. The threshing board, a most unlikely instrument for a worm or a dead person to use, was a flat piece of wood surrounded on the underside with teeth, a studded array of sharp stones, nails, or iron spikes. The language, figurative of course, presents God's way of eliminating the problems standing in the way of His redemptive program. Israel would pulverize her enemies, not in order to secure revenge on them for past deeds but rather to remove hindrances to her restoration to God's service in His redemptive plan for the world.

Only worthless chaff is blown away! The grain remains for God's storehouse! We should not interpret the prophet's words to mean an indiscriminate destruction of the nations. Only the enemies of God who are also Israel's enemies will be annihilated. Some of these will be found within Israel while some of God's people will be found to include non-Israelites. Spiritual Israel, the New Testament concept of Christians, existed even in Old Testament days. Only Israel within Israel, the true believers, represented God's true people!

This did not merely guarantee existence for national Israel—something much greater! She would rejoice in the victory which the Lord gave. Why? When the seventy returned to Jesus, excited because of their victory over those who opposed God's work, Jesus told them not to rejoice because the spirits were subject to them but "rejoice that your names are written in heaven" (Luke 10:20). Israel's greatest glory, as well as that of God's people in all generations, is that she had a part in bringing God's kingdom into being upon earth. This is something worth getting excited about! Not mere personal salvation and glorification but dedicated service is, after all, the greatest privilege we can possess!

A fourth and final truth rounds out the words of comfort to Israel. The prophet, with great pathos, recalled the present plight of the people and the miserable condition in which they were living at that time. He adapted his glorious promise to their actual need, giving a glowing description of the marvels that would take place in the desert journey, not losing sight of, however, the spiritual meaning of the experiences (41:17-20).

God's Resources Available

Realizing the people were in a condition of severe need from which they could not free themselves by human means, the prophet used appropriate language. Who were the perishing people? Where was the desolate place through which they would travel? We realize, of course, that the prophet spoke of crestfallen Israel in Exile and also of the destitute cities of Judah whose people had managed to eke out an existence since the fall of Jerusalem in 586 BC. However, we limit the prophet's message if we confine his words of comfort to these groups. The language is general, leaving room for a much wider application. God loves all people in all ages who have become wretched and weak because of sin. What about the journey? No airy, sentimental concept dominated the prophet's thinking. The people had a real trip before them across hostile country. So does every wicked person who journeys through the wilderness of sin.

In history, God was about to surpass the gracious acts He performed in the Exodus from Egypt. Expositors cannot be certain about the various trees listed in the text. All of them, however, were valuable and useful to the people in contrast to the harmful and useless thorns that characterized wilderness vegetation. The rivers, fountains, pools of water, and springs of water that God would provide were for more than the slaking of physical thirst. Water, throughout the Scriptures, stands as a symbol for both cleansing and spiritual refreshment. The transformation of the barren land would result in a complete reversal of conditions. The radical and all-embracing change would be a supernatural act, comparable to the spiritual salvation God would also provide for His people. When the prophet spoke of redemption, He implicitly referred also to a re-creation. All things would indeed become new!

Four strong, active verbs give the ultimate reason for God's demonstration of His power. He wished for the people to "see, and know, and consider, and understand" (v. 20) that a holy God was working through the people He had chosen. The almost unbelievable changes destined to take place in the near future would speak for themselves, testifying that the God of Israel never forsakes either His purpose or His people. Righteousness pervades every part of the prophet's message, including both rational and moral consistency, practical as well as theoretical faith, combined with the conscience of a reasonable plan implemented by the power to carry it through to a successful conclusion. Though the words have their shades of difference in meaning, holiness and righteousness come together in the person of Israel's God who loves His people and acts in history for their best interests.

III. Challenge (41:21-29)

Having shown that Israel's God possesses unlimited power and assured the people their redemption was imminent, the prophet turned his attention once more to those outside the nation. In his first address (41:1-7), he had hurled his words at those who worshiped the idols. In this one, he sent his challenge directly to the false gods, placing the words directly in the mouth of his God. Although scholars cannot agree as to the exact meaning of "former things" as contrasted with "things to come" (v. 22), the meaning of the prophet's words is clear. What have these idols done among the nations which worship them that they can set alongside Israel's record of what God has done in her midst? What promises did these nonentities ever make to their constituents that were fulfilled in history? What noble purposes did they ever conceive that were actually implemented? The gods had nothing to compare with what Israel's God possessed in the historical traditions of His people.

Inadequacy of Idols

Not only had the false gods failed to act in the past, they had no plan for the future. They offered no hope for the existing chaos of injustice and slavery which existed among the nations. If matters were left up to them, there would be no justice, peace, or joy brought to the defiled world. The prophet spoke caustically as he challenged the idols to do something, even if it were evil, to show they were alive. He spoke with disgust concerning those who chose to worship them. The idols of the pagan people were just as dead as Israel's God was alive! Let the false deities prove otherwise!

The Calling of Cyrus

Rather than being manipulated by the people as the idols were, Israel's God took charge of history and determined the course of events. To prove this the prophet returned to his earlier statement (41:2-4), reminding the people that Israel's God had chosen Cyrus and given him power to conquer his enemies. The "north" and "east" should give no problem unless one wants to be an absolute purist. Actually, the empire of Cyrus was so spread out at the time he conquered Babylon that we cannot be dogmatic about the direction from which Cyrus came. John Skinner, one of the ablest Old Testament scholars, gave a symbolic application of the terms, saying, "The terms are poetic; the north is the region of mystery, and the east the region of light." He then quickly added, "In point of fact Cyrus came from the northeast."

Did Cyrus actually call upon the Lord's name and, if so, in what sense? The historical writer recorded Cyrus as attributing his victories to Israel's God and stated that he said, "he hath charged me to build him a house in Jerusalem" (Ezra 1:2-3). How completely sincere Cyrus was in his devotion to the true God or how much difference this made in other areas of his life is not the question at this point. He did, at least in some sense, call upon the Lord and certainly fulfilled God's purposes through his decree and the implementation of it. The prophet's point was that Israel's God foretold of Cyrus and his work while the idols knew nothing and certainly said nothing of it in advance.

Above everything else, the Hebrew prophets contended, refusing ever to surrender or compromise on the point, that their God was sovereign, possessing all knowledge and all power. For this reason, though the Hebrew text is difficult and scholars have disagreed among themselves about the proper translation, we can safely say that the prophet, above everything else, was saying God was not merely the first but the only one to bring the message of good tidings to Jerusalem concerning the homecoming of their fellow Israelites who had been in captivity (41:27). On the other hand, none of the idols nor any of their devotees could serve as an adviser in the crisis confronting the nations. Why? Because they were products of the people. The Israelites believed in and worshiped a God who made persons in His image, but the pagans had created gods in their own image. Therein lies all the difference! Let God be God, and let human beings be human beings! The Lord God omnipotent reigneth! Let the world not only rejoice but obey! Both coins in the fountain of justice need to be kept before us constantly. God is and always shall be! Any who oppose Him or seek to usurp His position are doomed to defeat!

3
They Who Serve Are the Immortals
(42:1-25)

Of all people, prophets of God must be careful that those who hear them do not misunderstand! The Lord is all powerful and will, in time, destroy all His enemies. But why? Not merely to set up an arbitrary rule over them! Far from it! God's goal in history is to establish His sovereignty over all humankind because only as He rules completely can the world know a social order of justice, peace, and freedom. He does not desire merely a new power structure with the name of Yahweh replacing that of Marduk or another deity, but rather to clear the ground so that a government rooted in righteousness, and compassion can endure.

Thus far, in successive periods of Israel's history, God's Messiah has been presented under three major figures or concepts: Prophet, Priest, King! Now, the greatest emerges, one that does not necessarily exclude the others but adds a dimension that rounds off the idea and gives both quality and depth to the divine goal for human values. The Messiah will be a *Servant!*

Servant Poems

Most scholars agree four major "servant poems" can be found in this symphonic drama (42:1-9; 49:1-6; 50:4-9; 52:13 to 53:12). Progress takes place as the poem moves forward, but the servant is presented first as national Israel. Next, the prophet saw God's purpose being worked out through "Israel within Israel," the spiritual nucleus of the nation that responded affirmatively to God's will. Finally, however, the prophet made it clear that only an individual could consummate God's redemptive program, and he must be one who suffers vicariously. The ultimate fulfillment is, of course, Jesus Christ who, Paul said, "died for our sins according to the scriptures" (1 Cor. 15:3).

37

Meaning of Term

A title of honor, implying executive power in the king's name and by his authority, the term *servant* was considered a "royal plenipotentiary" among Israel's neighbors. The Hebrew root, however, meant a person at the disposal of another, responsible for carrying out his will. Thus the honor implied total and absolute obedience on the servant's part. Jeremiah and Ezekiel had already set forth the truth that all Israel was, in a sense, the servant of the Lord. The nation collectively was chosen to reveal God's holiness and, as she understood it and became mature enough to accept it, His mercy to the nations. Whatever conclusions may be reached later, we must see, at first, the corporate concept of Israel as God's original intention for His redemptive work.

I. Proclamation (42:1-9)

Persons cannot live creatively without ideals. Neither can God! He, through His prophet, presented the dream He had for the nation. He began it in Abraham and refused to relinquish His goal for Israel until she unequivocally showed Him she would not measure up to His expectations!

When the word *behold* occurs in prophetic literature, we stand upon the threshold of a great message. God is ready to introduce His servant to the world and announce his character so that all may recognize him. True, the prophet had addressed the nation as "servant" previously (41:8-9), but he was not, at that time, presenting him to the world in an official capacity. Now, however, God wanted everyone to see Israel for whom she was and desired for the nation herself to realize her identity. The characteristics set forth about her are true of any individual servant of God at any time. For this reason, every person can profit from the description, apply the ideals set forth to one's own life, and measure how well one feels one is pleasing God in one's own quest for spiritual maturity.

Traits of the Servant

Above everything else, any servant of the Lord must be anointed with and possessed by the divine Spirit, the breath of God which gives both meaning and motivation to life. Such a setting apart and filling will produce the characteristics necessary for those to qualify for the roles set out for them whom God chooses and in whom His entire being delights.

Chief among the functions is that of bringing a right way of living, designated by the all-inclusive Hebrew word *mishphat,* usually translated "justice" but implying entirety of fairness in relationships which enables people of different cultures to coexist until the time when they can share the same religious ideas and loyalties.

God's hidden sovereignty will become visible in the person of His Servant, but certain traits unrecognized by most as greatness will also prevail. First, God's servant will not call attention to himself. He will be vocally gentle and undemonstrative in manner. Second, rather than exploiting the weak for his own gain, the servant will gently fan the good that is in all human hearts and seek to develop it into God's ideal. Third, as he pursues rightness as a cosmic demand, he will hold fast to his integrity, knowing that the end never justifies the means. Faithfulness always remains as the essential quality for success in making an ideal become reality. Fourth, he will refuse to become disenchanted or lose heart as he moves into the larger world on his quest to bring all human-kind under the righteous rule of God's equity in personal relationships. He will keep constantly before himself the fact that the nations of the world, whether they realize it or not, are eagerly awaiting His mission. One recalls the testimony of a missionary that a group of heathens in Africa once said when they heard the story of Jesus, "We always knew there was someone like Him. You have only told us His name."

God's Method

In every generation, true servants of God have worked in this same unobtrusive manner. Glamorous self-assertion in high places of the world wins no real victories in the issues that matter. Silent spiritual influences best invade the soul and produce lasting results. Paradoxically, the canonical prophets, certainly not the pre-Exilic ones, cannot be said to have furnished the completely ideal example for the coming Servant. Perhaps the "still small voice" which spoke to Elijah best prefigured the Savior's ministry. Phillips Brooks caught the spirit:

> How silently, how silently
> The wondrous gift is givén!
> So God imparts to human hearts
> The blessings of his heavén.
>
> No ear may hear his coming,

But in this world of sin,
Where meek souls will receive him, still
The dear Christ enters in.

In both Old and New Testaments, the themes of creation and new creation stand parallel. The divine resources that brought the first world into being can and will bring another at the proper time, but can do more. The God who conquered chaos in the material realm and brought order can overcome the chaos of human lives in this present era. The prophet turned from announcing God's speech about His servant (vv. 1-4) and introduced His words to the servant (vv. 5-9). He used the definite article before the word for *deity,* stressing the contrast between the true God and false heathen ones. The word used for *spread forth* the earth means to beat out into a thin surface and combines the idea of density and extension. Although scientific research today enables us to know more about the expanding universe, the prophet's concepts are by no means incorrect. He conveyed his thought in terms of "beating out the earth" in the way that a silversmith makes a lump of silver expand until it is large enough to bend and so to form a bowl. The metaphor presents a picture which is by no means incorrect but shows remarkable knowledge and creative imagination for one of that day. Great is God's revelatory process! The prophet used "breath" and "spirit" in a nearly identical sense; the divine principle of life was breathed into mankind at creation.

A Further Word

God's affirmation that the servant, called in righteousness, will receive God's protection actually repeats what has already been said, but the assurance paves the way for a new statement. The servant has been chosen by God not for his own glorification but in order to bring the light of divine truth and love to the nations. Through the servant, the promise made to Abraham will be fulfilled. In the seed of Abraham, blessings shall go to the nations (Gen. 12:2).

When the prophet represented God as declaring that one function of His Servant was "to open the blind eyes" (v. 7), the statement was equivalent to saying He would impart instruction to the ignorant. He would acquaint them with God's truth and way of deliverance. The Scriptures often picture those in the world as in darkness and thus blinded. In this condition, people do not see their true character or condition. They, therefore, need someone to "enlighten, sanctify, and

save" them. Likewise, "to bring out the prisoners from the dungeon, and
. . . prison-house" refers to spiritual deliverance from the confinement
and enslavement that sin brings. To breathe the pure air of forgiven sin
brings a freedom equal and even superior to any release from an earthly
prison no matter how wretched and miserable. Bernard of Clairvaux was
right when he said:

> But what to those who find? ah! this,
> No tongue nor pen can show
> The love of Jesus, what it is
> None but his loved ones know.

Turning from the servant directly to the people, the Lord assured them
that He is the only true God and has no intention of surrendering His
sovereignty or even sharing it with another person or thing who claims
the power of deity. One's name in the Scriptures, especially the Old
Testament, always stands for one's character, and Israel's God kept
before the people constantly the name by which He had revealed Himself
to Moses. The fact of being or essential existence was another truth that
might also have been implicit in this name. As the supreme truth of the
Christian gospel is that "Jesus lives," so the Israelites of Old Testament
days could rejoice to know that their God possessed life in unique
contrast to that of any other deity which the nations held in superstitious
awe. For that reason, no true prophet could ever compromise his message by allowing even token recognition of these "not gods" which
dominated the life of Israel's neighbors. The Decalogue said it well, "I
am the Lord your God and I tolerate no rivals" (Ex. 20:5, GNB).

II. Praise (42:10-12)

When majestic thoughts crowd in on us and fill our souls so profoundly that we "run out of words," a song usually finds its way to our lips.
So with the prophets! Several of the highly elevated prose passages in the
apostle Paul's writings are thought to have been songs used by the early
church in their worship liturgy. How natural that after describing the
Lord's servant and his work, the prophet should sing a song about what
he had just proclaimed!

A New Song

Since he had spoken of old things having been fulfilled and new things
that would come, the prophet commanded that the rejoicing of praise be

a "new song" and that all the earth hear it. In fact, some scholars feel
verse 9, in the preceding section, belongs more appropriately with the
verses that speak of praising God and giving glory to His name to the
farthest end of the earth. What is involved in "the former things" we
cannot be certain, but the prophet mentioned several times that the
victories of Cyrus and his mighty act of deliverance had been foretold.
How far in advance? By how many spokesmen? In how much detail?
These will always remain a mystery unless some new evidence is discovered, but an old dispensation had certainly passed away, and the
Babylonian Exodus was so significant in Israel's history that only a "new
song" could express its tremendous effect upon the nation.

Of course, the word *new* does not always convey the idea of excellence
and beauty in distinction from common and ordinary, but, because of the
subject with which this new song deals, no other word can properly
describe it. This song was not new in contrast to songs sung to idols. In
fact, we have no convincing evidence that worshipers ever sang praises
to the lifeless things that were a part of their ritual. Rather, this new song
would be a tribute to the redemption that God had worked in the life
of the nation and which prefigured, though they did not fully understand
at that time, the spiritual freedom from sin that the ultimate Messiah
would bring.

To Everyone Everywhere

What was the scope of this melodious praise? How far would it go?
These God-glorifying songs were to go "from one end of the earth to
another," and several specific categories are mentioned. Traders, naviga-
tors, merchants, seamen—these not only stand for those in commerce
implying that business would be redeemed through the justice that Messiah would bring, but another thought is present. The conversion of those
who travel the seas would have an important effect in diffusing true
religion to the distant nations. The missionary message of God's grace
is present in abundance throughout the Hebrew Scriptures. God has
always wanted the whole world to know of His redemptive love. The
most moving hymns we sing in the Christian faith are those that urge
us to tell the story of Jesus to the world.

Since a large percentage of the world population, especially in that
day, lived on islands, the prophet mentioned these people particularly.
He included also the uninhabited places called *wilderness,* but this word

can be misleading. Actually the word means the most uncultivated countries, implying that even the most rude and barbarous people would rejoice when they heard of God's mercy in Jesus Christ. The cities were where masses of people congregate and live in crowded conditions. Small villages such as Kedar, probably a pastoral tribe of the Syrian desert, and isolated places such as Sela, most likely Petra in Edom, would find occasion for jubilant singing when the message reached them of the Messiah who brings forgiveness from sin. All are to lift their voices in testimony to God's redemption. As the last song in the Jewish hymn-book says, "Praise the Lord, all living creatures! Praise the Lord" (Ps. 150:6, GNB).

III. Purpose (42:13-17)

The basic reason for singing praises to the Lord precedes this section (42:9), but two others follow. Shouting and yelling could be heard as the prophet anticipated God rescuing His people from the powers of evil. Some scholars feel verse 13 more properly belongs with the preceding paragraph as the true reason for the nation's rejoicing. Though there is some merit for such a position, especially since the literary style remains in the third person, changing to first person only in verse 14, this picture of God attacking wickedness seems more a part of His further intention to bring His people home from captivity by removing all the difficulties that stood in their way.

A Hero God

The Lord comes across as a hero, stirred with zeal, raising His voice, and striking with fury against His enemies which are also the foes of Israel. Often, in the Old Testament, God enters the arena of conflict to defend His cause against those who would overthrow it. The image of His rushing on impetuously to take vengeance against those who would destroy His redemptive work was designed to encourage Israel by assuring them of God's fixed determination to deliver them from their bondage even though it had been brought about by their own stubbornness and wicked conduct. Implicit in all such passages is the truth of God's avowed purpose to make Himself known to all nations both as a holy Person and a compassionate Savior.

About to Give Birth

Next, God spoke directly to the people, using a daring image to suggest the nearness of the new day. He appeared as a woman about to give birth. The child was the "new things" that were about to appear. For a long time, God had been patient and allowed His opponents to carry the field. Now, however, He was ready to spring into action. Those translators who render "gasp and pant" rather than "destroy and devour" (v. 14) are probably nearer to the idea of the prophet since he was using the metaphor of a woman in labor. The "cry" could, however, refer to God's disapproval at the injustices done to Israel, whether in the context of a warrior in attack or a prospective mother in anguish. The prophet continued in the next verse with a motif of destruction against all who opposed God's purpose in redeeming His people. God would reverse the usual order of nature to allow the captives to return. This great metamorphosis of nature would remove all difficulties from the path of the people, both natural barriers and human armies. Both thoughts seem to be implicit in the prophet's words. The radical nature of the change emphasizes divine activity. No human strength or skill could work so mightily in behalf of a nation.

Opposition Must Be Destroyed

Laying waste the cultivated fields of one's enemy was the customary approach of a conquerer. By drying up the grains and fruits on which they depended for support, the foe would be rendered helpless. God was determined to work out His purpose for Israel regardless of what He must do to those who opposed the returning exiles. One translator renders, "Rivers I am going to turn into sandbanks, pools I shall render dry" (v. 15). The prophet wanted the people to know God would bring to desolation all who in their ignorant idol worship sought to oppose His redemptive purpose. Everything in their religious system—temples, altars, shrines—would be turned over and demolished. Whatever figure of speech he used and however he moved from one to another, the thought was the same. God could no longer bear the growing abomination of those pagan people who opposed Him. They must either be evangelized or destroyed. Of course, as always, God preferred to destroy their religious systems by bringing better ones to them.

God's purpose now comes to light! As in God's call to Jeremiah, a plucking up, breaking down, overthrowing, and destroying of the old

order must take place before a building and planting could come. Therefore, judgment of enemies must precede grace, both to Israel and to
others who would become God's people. The "blind" are, of course,
those who lack spiritual understanding even as the "deaf" mentioned
later are those who refuse to hear God's message. The picture of a total,
radical, and all-embracing change now comes in different figures. Although the primary reference in all of this passage was to the return from
Babylonian Exile, the thought is not limited to this event. God will
remove the darkness that prevents spiritual perception from all who will
submit to His leadership.

God Will Lend

When they travel, those who are blind have double difficulty. Subjec-
tively, their lack of vision hinders them, but objectively they cannot see
rough road ahead with all of its problems and hindrances. Literally, God
would deal with the natural adversities when necessary, but, even more
important, He would give strength for the returning Israelites to bear the
suffering that comes because their enemies will use every resource at their
command to bring hardships upon them. Judgment and mercy always
go together. God's coming will put terror to the enemies of righteousness, but it also will bring comfort and spiritual blessings to those who
put their trust in Him. The presence of God will turn darkness into light
and give strength for weakness.

The prophet voiced God's word that He would not leave them without
help for their journey, both the physical one across the desert and the
spiritual pilgrimage they traveled as they moved in their quest for a fuller
knowledge of His purpose for their lives. The magnitude of the work is
so great as to be unbelievable. Indeed, with persons such a goal is
impossible to realize. God, however, will not fail nor forget. One translator renders His words, "These are the things. I have done them and I
have not given them up." All of it, however, is not in the past. The tenses
have the thrust of a prophetic perfect. The divine messenger was so sure
God would do it that he spoke as though it were already accomplished.

No "Quick Fix"

One final word needs to be said concerning those who seek guidance
for their lives in non-existent gods. Too often, a person does not worship
something or someone because of a sane and sensible consideration of

possible alternatives. Rather, one chooses an object for one's affections that promises an immediate satisfaction, a sort of "quick fix" for what ails a person. In this manner, some modern-day cults and even immature Christians who "go crazy" over leaders with great charisma resemble those who worshiped idols in Old Testament days.

What will happen to those who make such things their trust and allegiance? Most translations render the two verbs as "turned back" and "ashamed," but an interesting nuance is present in both words. The first has as one of its meanings that of sliding back or as we say today becoming a backslider. Is this not always true of those whose concept of God is inadequate, usually entirely too shallow. Unless we serve a God big enough to challenge our mature loyalties, we will not "hold out" long in our religious life. So much of modern religion is a "flitting about" from one religious fad to another. This reflects to a large degree the idolatrous mind with a small or limited god.

The other verb, usually translated "ashamed," has more properly the idea of disappointment. In any day, those who run after every new fanciful innovation in religion will sooner or later be disappointed. What is the connection between "ashamed" and "disappointed" that would cause the same word to be translated either way? We are ashamed of someone when we are disappointed in them—we expected something better! One judgment God sends in this life for sin is our sense of shame when we realize the folly of what we have done. As people find their manufactured religious cures give no real protection, their conscious guilt will grow, producing a frustration that will sink even deeper into a neurotic state of depression. Such persons continue to grow more disenchanted and eventually become bitter with all religion. Only a great transforming act of God's grace can put them back on the road to forgiveness and joy. This is, of course, what God wished and planned for Israel and the nations if they would respond to Him!

IV. Plea (42:18-25)

The scene changes! A new mood took hold of the prophet. God spoke through him but no longer to announce impending judgment and salvation. Rather, the prophet turned his attention to the Israel of that day whom he saw as completely unprepared for her future task. One scholar called the earlier picture of the servant, Israel (vv. 1-4), an "ideal reality" and this one (vv. 18-20) an "empirical reality." Although this entire section seems to be a scathing denunciation, and indeed in some sense it is, a warmhearted invitation seems to be present even within the context of severe rebuke. The prophet invited, even urged, Israel twice to take a good look at herself. He began, "Hear, ye deaf; and look, ye blind, that ye may see" (42:18) while later in the same passage he asked, "Who is there among you that will give ear to this? that will hearken and hear for the time to come?" (42:23) Implicit within every prophetic condemnation is an invitation, a proposition from God that forgiveness is available upon the basis of true repentance (Jer. 18:7-8).

Israel's Greater Guilt

Of course, the present, pitiable plight of Israel was self-evident. Short-sightedness and disobedience to the divine will had brought it about. Though the Gentile world was enslaved by ignorance and stupidity, Israel stood even more guilty. Blessed of God, she possessed the law and prophets as a religious guide and God's redemptive acts in history as the constraining motivation for righteous conduct. She had, however, chosen to ignore them. The nation seemed to be emotionally incapable of realizing her own history was a unique visitation from God which, therefore, presented moral and ethical obligations. She had become spiritually color blind, unable to distinguish the true issues of the day. The prophet summarized it graphically, "Who is so blind as the one who holds my commission, so deaf as the servant of the Lord? You have seen much but remembered little, your ears are wide open but nothing is heard" (42:19-20, NEB).

Not for a moment would the prophet have anyone assume God did His work reluctantly. Eagerly and enthusiastically, God revealed His will that Israel might enjoy the good life that comes through obedience and serve as a vehicle for making it known to the nations of the world. Tragedy of all tragedies, the honored nation had refused to accept her mission! Instead of seeking others and telling of the good news, she now was a prisoner waiting for others to seek her out and set her free! Israel's condition at this time paralleled one of her earlier rulers who, in one of his literary masterpieces, lamented, perhaps autobiographically, "They made me keeper of the vineyards; But mine own vineyard have I not kept" (Song of Sol. 1:6).

A Realistic Assumption

Few pictures of desolation equal the prophet's words about Babylon in Exile. Though some Old Testament passages seem to imply the Babylonians treated the Jews with a certain amount of kindness, we should not doubt for one moment that the words in this context were not, to a large extent, literal. Robbed and plundered, they surely were! Though some translators would edit the text a bit and give a slightly different meaning to soften the tribulation, the phrase "snared in holes" seems to best parallel "hid in prison houses" although we cannot rule out completely the Syriac rendering, "All their youth are snared" which is a legitimate translation of the Hebrew. An uncertain and uneasy existence certainly prevailed. Israel saw no one at hand to serve as a deliverer. Only God could provide this messiah and the prophet insisted, at every possible opportunity, that God *would* supply one and indeed had already done so in Cyrus, the Persian general who did not realize the full implication of his gracious act in allowing the Jews to return home.

An Urgent Plea

More than a rhetorical question, the prophet's words in verse 23 expressed his earnest desire for at least some of the people to realize the significance of their relationship to Israel's covenant God and make preparation for the national deliverance by being a part of the spiritual nucleus that He could use in His redemptive purpose. Some have considered the prophet's words similar to Absalom's "Oh that I were made judge in the land, that every man who hath any suit or cause might come unto me, and I would do him justice!" (2 Sam. 15:4) or David's "Oh that one would give me water to drink of the well of Bethlehem, which is by the gate!" (2 Sam. 23:15). The format is not, of course, exactly the same, but both of these longings were actually invitations. Absalom wanted the people to make him their monarch, and the hearers of David, whether he meant them to do so or not, interpreted their leader's wish as a command. At least, they risked their lives to secure the water for him! The prophet certainly wanted the people to respond to his wish and return to God! The three verbs in the parallelism do not seem to contain any particular shades of meaning or nuances that would imply a progressive buildup in zeal, but the repetition certainly indicates an intense desire by the prophet for his invitation to be heeded.

A Serious Warning

Though some might feel the prophet's final words represent an anticlimax after such a heartwarming and compassionate invitation, such is not necessarily true. Warnings are always proper, especially when dealing with such a rebellious people. Reminders are always relevant. The present tragic condition of Israel should have caused her to contemplate the cause and act with wisdom. The prophet identified himself with the generation who had sinned, but he also reminded the people that past generations were also guilty. Judgment had not come without warning! When the Canaanites abused the land, God had given it to Joshua and the people of his day. When Israel's theocracy failed because of the people's disobedience, God permitted a kingdom. When it fell apart, God allowed foreigners to spoil the land. He, however, gave Judah and Jerusalem fair warning by letting them see the Northern Kingdom go down first. Still, they would not listen! The people were without excuse!

The enigma of Israel's history was that she saw God give her over to enemies and yet was unable to understand the meaning of her calamities. Prophetic warnings seemed to make no impression upon the people. The question was now whether or not this period in her history would be an exception. She did not learn from the Egyptian Exodus. Would she learn from the Babylonian deliverance? Had she become so hardened that she could make no response, or was there still hope? Even when God's zeal was burnt into her bones, she failed to realize why or understand the significance. Punishment did not motivate! Would the grace of national deliverance accomplish that which national disgrace had not done? What would it take to lead God's servant to assume the role He had chosen for her? The prophet stood perplexed, but he kept on trying!

A Relevant Word

Leaving ancient Israel for a moment, let us reflect on an eternal truth suggested by this passage which is appropriate for all generations. Have we in our day caught the spirit of servanthood any more than they? When the Salvation Army celebrated the one-hundredth anniversary of its founder's birthday, William Booth, the centennial edition of their publication, *The War Cry,* had a sentence in one of its articles that should etch itself in our memory, "William Booth, king among men so long as men count service the badge of royalty." Danger stalks throughout the world too alarmingly for anything worth preserving to be safe unless we develop a generation of devoted men and women who are completely self-giving. Any person who realizes how critical our situation and whose eye is open to the need must agree with Dorothea Beale, pioneer of women's education, who said, "Service is the rent we pay for our room on earth." Even a skeptic like Renan insisted that "the stability of our institutions turns upon the amount of sacrifice that is built into them."

As surely as God called ancient Israel to be His servant, every person who knows the true "Servant of God" as Lord and Savior is called upon for full commitment to His Kingdom's purposes. No one who has put his hand to the plow should even think about looking back. The need is too great, the opportunities too many, and the joy of dedication too fulfilling! The life of service brings blessings in abundance. We can't afford to miss it!

4
How Dare You Doubt the One Who Has Done All!
(43:1 to 44:28)

Any person who seeks to present a homiletically-oriented exposition of Isaiah 40—55 faces the realistic fact that a clear-cut analytical approach by subject matter is virtually impossible. One scholar spoke of the "interlocking of themes"—an excellent way to state the case. The first three chapters give the message of the prophet in three clear-cut steps, yet each chapter builds solidly on the previous one and depends upon it for background to be correctly understood.

Although not all interpreters agree, I have chosen the next two chapters (43:1 to 44:28) as a block to be considered for study. Some feel 42:18-25 should be considered part of chapter 43 while others feel 44:24-28 should be presented in connection with chapter 45. Both of these contentions are not without merit because each chapter of the prophet's symphonic message feeds into the other, and of course no chapter divisions were present in the original text. Nevertheless, one must make a decision and stay with it. I shall, therefore, consider the material according to this format.

Israel, Exiled and Delivered

Thus far, the main thrust of the prophet's message has been a contrast between the ideal and actual Israel. In this passage, however, he moves to a distinction between Israel in the misery of Exile and Israel in the glory of its coming deliverance. Though the people have sinned, the Lord will not cast them off, but a bright future is about to dawn for them. They must, however, recognize who it is that blesses them and be willing to forsake any worship of other deities, giving full allegiance to their God and assuming the redemptive role He has chosen for them. A brief analysis of the two chapters will help lay the foundation for spiritual truths to be gleaned.

Analysis of the Material

In the first section (43:1-7), the prophet announced that God was about to redeem Israel. Not only those in Babylon, but Israelites from all places would be restored. They belonged to the Lord in a special way and were brought into being by God for the purpose of accomplishing His work. Next (43:8-13), God calls all peoples, Jews and Gentiles, as witnesses. The nations were called upon to produce evidence of the power they claim for their gods. Israel, though not without shortcomings, was told to testify of her God's great resources and grace.

The third section (43:14-21) tells how God would destroy Babylon, making possible another great exodus, surpassing the one from Egypt. The fourth (43:22-28), a passage similar to 42:18-25, points out that though Israel had sinned against God during Exilic days, forfeiting all claim to His love, He had forgiven them. The next chapter opens with a section (44:1-5) that tells how God will pour out His Spirit upon the people, blessing and prospering them so much that other nations would voluntarily join the favored nation.

The sixth division (44:6-20) contains perhaps the most blistering condemnation of idolatry to be found in the Bible. Preceded by a reassertion and demonstration of God's timelessness and sovereignty (vv. 6-8), the prophet set forth a complete and remorseless exposure of how irrational is one who worships things made with hands. A final word (44:21-28) urges Israel to lay to heart all things God had said to them through His prophet and calls for both heaven and earth to celebrate the wonders of Israel's redemption. The reference to Cyrus (44:28) serves as a transition to the next major section of the book (45:1-25) but is definitely a part of the material in these chapters.

Though some of these sections may have, at one time, had an independent existence apart from the unit as it now stands, the prophet has put the material together artistically, forming a monograph on the greatness of God and the thoroughness of His redemptive work. We shall use one "key word" for each section to serve as a thematic suggestion around which to gather the material as we seek for the fuller, more comprehensive message.

I. Salvation (43:1-7)

Since the language the prophet used had no present, past, or future tense as such but rather a perfect tense for completed action and an imperfect tense for incompleted action, we have a problem at times knowing whether the prophet spoke of something that had happened or something that would happen. The "prophetic perfect" is when the speaker was so sure something will happen that he spoke of it as an accomplished fact. The "have redeemed" (43:1) could refer, of course, to the Egyptian bondage, but probably the prophet saw the actual leaving of Babylon as an event about to be accomplished and spoke of it as having been done. Perhaps the decree of Cyrus had been given and preparations were being made. The perfect tense means the prophet saw it in his mind's eye as a completed action. The promises that follow are imperfects, something not yet done, but the prophet did not stress them quite as forcefully as he did the fact that Israel would leave Babylon. This does not mean he had any doubt God would be with the returning exiles as they passed through the waters or walked through the fire, but rather he emphasized more strongly the leaving of Babylon.

Jacob and Israel

Thirteen times within chapters 40—48 the prophet used the double designation of Jacob and Israel and, with only one exception (41:8), in that order. Jacob the deceiver in the Genesis story had to become Israel the prince before God could use him. Perhaps the prophet was alluding to the fact, in nuance, that the "Jacob" character must be abandoned in order for the nation to fulfill her role as God's servant. In spite of this use of names, however, God addressed the people tenderly and in the singular which gives a personal if not intimate appeal.

Through Deepest Trouble

As we study the Hebrew prophets, we should remember that God's spokesmen always addressed their contemporaries through a historical situation of pain and sorrow while interpreting its meaning and significance. The prophet did not deceive Israel about sufferings that awaited her, but nevertheless he promised God's presence would always serve as the source of strength for passing through the "fire" and the "waters," a double metaphor for perilous situations. In fact, these two contingencies represent the extremities of adversity which confront humankind. Whatever might arise to frustrate and hinder, God would supply their need and help them to emerge victorious!

Closely connected with the redemption concept is always that of a ransom. The "mousetrap" theory of the atonement, which insisted God paid Satan a ransom, dominated Christian theology for nearly a thousand years. Here, the prophet introduced this idea by stating God paid a ransom for Israel. He gave to Persia three countries in Africa as a compensation for allowing Israel to go free. Seba was probably a northern province of Ethiopia, lying between the White and Blue Nile.

Redemption and Substitution

Though some scholars have objected violently to such a concept, we should remember that the idea of substitution was deeply ingrained in the concept of Israel's religion. Under the Mosaic law, one redeemed one's own possession by paying a price, the offering of a substitute. The prophets always spoke in terms that their audience could understand. Ezekiel made a similar statement when he portrayed God giving Nebuchadnezzar the land of Egypt in compensation for his labor against Tyre which he did not receive.

How are we to understand the prophet's words to Israel? For one thing—and this is very important—we are dealing with poetical concepts. The prophet was saying that, in God's eyes, Israel was worth more than all the other nations. Why? Not because He loved Israel more but because He had chosen her for a redemptive mission and, therefore, was blessing her in a unique way. Unless we understand this truth, we miss the idea of God's great love for Israel. She was His servant, to bring the principles of revealed religion to the nations in order that God might unite the world through His Messiah. This is the only valid reason for saying that Israel was God's chosen people!

Don't Be Afraid!

One minister claims to have counted and found the expression "fear not," or a similar phrase, occurring 365 times in the Bible. He remarks, "One for every day of the year." Whatever else God does for His people, He seeks constantly to assure them of His presence—the greatest antidote known to anxiety and uneasiness about the future. Though the people faced what seemed to be insuperable difficulties, God's redemption would be so unbelievably wondrous that they should take comfort and renew their courage.

What about the gathering of God's seed from the various places? We do not know to how many different locales the people fled in the overthrow of the two kingdoms in 722 and 586 BC. Nor do we know, for instance, what Assyria did with the captives she took. She probably kept some nearby, but, no doubt, many were deported to other vassal states. Jewish people did not amalgamate easily, especially the more loyal who were probably the ones taken by Assyria unlike the ones she left in the land of Israel. The prophets spoke several times of how God would scatter the people to other locations. Only a moment's serious reflection will make one realize that history is fluid, and such catastrophic events as the destruction of Samaria and Jerusalem would result in a general dispersion even though the bulk of the people might have gone to Assyria and Babylon. Often, in pre-Exilic history, the Israelites were conquered by their neighbors and various captives taken. All of these peoples would have been included in the prophet's promise of a general restoration.

Why Did God Do It?

What was the purpose? Israel was still a corporate nation. Though the Northern Kingdom had been cut to pieces and the Southern Kingdom moved almost as a group to Babylon and some to Egypt, the covenant with Abraham promised Israel would be a blessing to the world. She could not perish until she has accomplished the task assigned her. We cannot say with intellectual integrity that the people repented. True, Moses (Deuteronomy 30:1-3) had foreseen the people's captivity and promised they would be restored when they sought the Lord with all their heart, but God's deliverance of the people was so that His redemptive work could be carried on rather than because of a wholesale repentance on their part. This is where the parallel fails when we seek to make Israel's restoration a "type" of the Christian's salvation today. God restored Israel because of His grace and to bring glory to Himself by the redemptive work He would accomplish through them.

II. Summons (43:8-13)

The courtroom format fascinated Israel's prophets. They often called the people into an imaginary scene where the Lord's case was presented in a judicial setting. In this section, witnesses were summonsed to testify concerning the one upon whom they depended for national security and personal guidance. God asked any of the nations to step forward and recount any divine guidance they had received or produce any evidence of power they saw for their gods. When they were unable to show they had been blessed with supernatural wisdom or that their idols were worthy of confidence, God called upon His servant Israel.

Which God Can Foretell?

Blind and deaf though she was, the prophet felt Israel still had the capacity of vision and thus he confronted her with her calling. Monotheism dominated every message to Israel as well as to the nations. This was the issue! Are there many gods or one? If there are many deities, morals are relative. No absolute exists, and life is one wild race of indulgence and selfishness. Whichever god wins at a particular time dominates and his concept of values prevails. If as the prophet insisted however, Yahweh is the sole Creator and Redeemer, two facts cannot be denied. First, His purpose and plan will be ultimately victorious. His essential goal in history is that all people everywhere will hear of Him, believe in Him, and become subject to His lordship. This was of course not fulfilled until Jesus stepped into history, but the truth is implicit in this passage. Second, all ethical conduct must be judged in the light of His holiness. Idolatry produced immoral abuses of all types, but the worship of one God who is rooted and grounded in ethical righteousness saw morality as a cosmic demand.

Nature of Prophecy

The claim of Israel's God to have declared events before they happened poses a problem for expositors. For example, how long in advance did the prophets, speaking for God, reveal the deliverance and especially the appearance of Cyrus in history as God's instrument for granting the exiles permission to return. One group of scholars insist the prophet always spoke to his contemporaries about issues of that day and thus contend any prediction was shortly before the event took place and was based on the keen insight the prophet possessed, illuminated of course by his spiritual fellowship with God.

More conservative scholars, such as Edward J. Young, thought Isaiah of the eighth century saw all of these events a century and a half before they occured and wrote a great symphonic drama in order that the people of later days could read and take courage that their God had planned the captivity and deliverance from the beginning. Young said without apology, "We have adopted the position that Isaiah, toward the close of his active ministry in the latter days of the reign of Hezekiah, looked forward in the Spirit of prophecy to the time when his people, disobedient to God . . . would go away in physical captivity to Babylon." He continued, "This deep bondage . . . was no cause for fear, however, for God had paid the price to redeem and set free the people. As a sign of that deliverance there was to be the return to Palestine from Exile, but the return was only a sign. The real redemption would be accomplished at a later time, when God Himself would offer up His only begotten Son."

The issue of authorship will not be settled upon such evidence as literary style, including the use of similar words in both sections of the book but rather upon one's concept of the nature of inspiration and how God worked in the prophet's mind. For our exposition, however, we must understand the message to Israel at this point in her history was that Israel's God, revealed as Yahweh, is the only true God, and no one existed before Him, nor will there be anyone after Him to compete for His position as Lord of history. Of all nations, Israel should be a witness of that fact even as a Christian who has met this God in Jesus Christ can give testimony from personal experience in redemption through the One who died on the cross and rose again.

Do Not Doubt God!

Nothing in the religion of the nations threw any light upon history nor gave persons any basis for finding their personal identity or future movement toward a goal. It is the same in any generation. Those who contend for a relativism, pluralism, or even a blatant atheism should consider carefully the words of the one who said so penetratingly, "When the microscopic search of infidelity has found one square mile on this earth where human life is held in due regard, where old age is honored, where womanhood is respected and infant life is cared for, that the Gospel of Jesus Christ did not go there first and lay the foundation of civilization that made these things possible, it will be in order for our skeptical friends and all others who deny the truth to move there and propogate and ventilate their views." Polytheism makes impossible the unity of life that is essential to man's emotional health. The prophet pressed his hearers to face the facts about Israel's God honestly as one would in a court of justice. Let each side come with their evidence and choose, by the preponderence of proof, which is the living God. Then, in the words of Elijah, "If the Lord is God, worship him" (1 Kings 18:21, GNB).

Come to court! Give your testimony! Hear the evidence and make your decision!

III. Spectaculars (43:14-21)

Another argument for the safety of God's people, as presented by the prophet, was the great acts of the Lord on their behalf. In chapters 40 through 55 of this book, the prophet called Israel's God by the name of *Redeemer* more than all the Old Testament passages combined. By joining it with the term *Holy One of Israel,* the thought is projected that God does not compromise His righteousness in order to deliver His people. His holiness demands that sin be punished, but, in the work of His servant, holiness and mercy meet and both are satisfied. Paul spoke of how the atoning work of God's greatest and ultimate Servant, Jesus Christ, makes it possible for God to be both just and the Justifier of those who believe (Romans 3:26).

Down with Babylon!

What had God done or what would He do in order to redeem His people? First, He would deal with Babylon. Although the Hebrew text of verse 14 presents some problems, Delitzsch was probably correct when he said that none of the proposed alterations "effect any improvement" upon the traditional translations. In order to redeem Israel, God would throw down Babylon with all of her pride. In their haste to escape, many of the people would take refuge in their ships which had been the source of their jubilant self-confidence. Favorably situated on the Euphrates with access to the Persian Gulf, Babylon had become a commercial and naval power. After Cyrus took Babylon, we read very little of the nation's commerce. The soldiers diverted the Euphrates from its course in order to enter the city, spreading it over the adjacent country. To prevent invasion from that river again, later Persian kings obstructed navigation by building dams across the Tigris and Euphrates.

These facts confirm the translation that appears in the traditional versions rather than those who amend the text and render "fugitives" as "bolts" (v. 14) which would stand symbolically for nobles or literally for parts of the gates of the city. Herodotus, the Greek historian, described freight ships unloading in Babylon, and we know from other sources that Babylonian ships navigated both the Euphrates and Persian Gulf, employing vessels built by the Phoenicians for warlike purposes, thus making "hurling to the ground" of the ships a logical statement. Also, Herodotus spoke of the ships on the Euphrates as "ships of rejoicing," a phrase identical with that of the prophet. The passage certainly rests upon a solid historical basis.

A Second Exodus

The sequel to Babylon's overthrow is of course the deliverance of Israel, compared to the greatest miracle in Israel's past history, the Exodus from Egypt. Although the prophet clearly seemed to mean the miracle at the Red Sea when he spoke of a "way in the sea" and a "path in the mighty waters" (v. 16) several have suggested that he referred to how Cyrus entered the city of Babylon by the Euphrates that ran through the center of the great metropolis. Attractive as this hypothesis is and as dramatic as the entry of Cyrus must have been between the walls either on dry ground or in a river made shallow by rerouting much of it, one feels the prophet referred directly to the victory of Pharaoh especially in light of the next verse which speaks of the "chariot and horse, the army and the mighty man" (v. 17) followed by the exhortation to "Remember . . . not the former thing, neither consider the things of old" (43:18).

God was about to act with a new spectacular! He would do something greater than dry up the Red Sea. Where He once made a sea become dry ground, now He would make a desert become a river. Streams in the desert! God would provide for His people! Though it would be a new act, it should not have been a surprise. God had blessed His people and delivered them from every crisis. This new deliverance would grow organically from the old as the butterfly develops from the caterpillar. God would make a new route—not through the sea as in the Exodus but over the wilderness that separated Babylonia from Palestine.

Nothing Can Stop God!

Though we have no reason to doubt for one moment that God protected the people from wild and ferocious animals, the prophet's words have an even more cosmic significance significance. They stand for anything or person that would seek to hinder God's people and His purpose in redemption. Anything that militates against God's loving and creative goals in history must be dealt with in such a way that the nations have no doubt the Lord is on the side of His people. Why did God perform

these great demonstrations of His power and grace? He wished to preserve the remembrance of His name and transmit the knowledge to
future generations. The people, both present and those to come later,
would celebrate His goodness. By being restored to their land, they
would demonstrate they were God's people, chosen for a special service.
Every manifestation of God's mighty power has an ethical motive. He
wished the people to realize justice must prevail if mankind is to live
together in peace and harmony.

IV. Sins (43:22-28)

The prophet paused to draw back the curtain on the pain which was
in the Father's heart. The people needed to face a tragic fact. For seventy
years, the nation in Exile had been blind to the underlying purpose of
God. They actually confronted the ideal as the prophet set forth a string
of negatives to point out how Israel not only failed to declare the praise
of God but had actually grown tired of Him. Scholars differ concerning
the not bringing of sacrifices in the first part of verse 23. Does this mean
literally the people did not bring any, rationalizing perhaps that, because
they were away from the Temple, they were not required to do so? Or
did the prophet mean "there was no true bringing" of offerings and what
the people did render was a "sham offering" and not the "real thing"?
The technical difference is, of course, not important. The prophet was
condemning them for failing to keep alive their loyalty to the religious
ideal that had characterized their faith since the beginning of their
spiritual quest when God made it clear He had chosen them for a special
mission to the nations of the world. The much-disputed statement that
God had not "burdened thee with offerings, nor wearied thee with frank-
incense" (43:23b) does not mean that He had exempted them from any
duty of bringing sacrifices but rather that He had not imposed a weari-
some burden that produced no spiritual profit. The prophet immediately
voiced a further charge: their failure to bring an abundance of offerings.
The expression "bought me no sweet cane" uses a play on words with
the noun being very similar in sound. The "fat of thy sacrifices" is
translated by some in such a way as to suggest the people had not
"drenched" the Lord with their gifts.

Love Conquers All

God's mercy and grace break through the condemnation. The one against whom Israel has transgressed might well have never been expected to forgive. But He did! The Hebrew text shocks us with its emphasis—I, I, He! Verse 25 emphasizes that God alone was the one who forgave. He wiped out that which was recorded against Israel so it could never be seen again. Why? God said that it was for His sake. Although some have emphasized that it was so the nations would have no grounds for claiming He was a weak God who could not protect His people, and there is some merit in that position, the meaning is even deeper. He had a job for Israel, the one for which he called Abraham in the first place. The Redeemer would come though the nation. In fact, personal and national forgiveness was not granted at the expense of justice and honor. The Suffering Servant's vicarious atonement, to be revealed later, would make such vindication possible. The miracle of God's forgiveness was the miracle that would liberate Israel from her bondage and create a new Israel with a new future. The prophet at this point was not so concerned with individual salvation, although that was never absent from his message, but rather he sought to stress that a nucleus from national Israel would form the spiritual kernel to carry on God's redemptive mission when they returned home.

Present Your Case!

Having mixed his condemnation with assurance of forgiveness, the prophet returned to his basic thesis and portrayed a court scene once more. This time God and Israel were adversaries with Israel called upon to "set forth thy cause that thou mayest be justified" (43:26b). God's command for the people to "put [Him] in remembrance" may be a play on words from His previous statement that He would "not remember" their sins, thus containing a bit of irony. The nation could bring any works of merit they felt they possessed in order to refute God's charge against them. "Let us plead together" is the verb form which produces the noun "justice." God will never be guilty of being unfair. He wants right to prevail and was willing to listen to any reasonable plea Israel had on her behalf.

Though unwilling to browbeat Israel, God at the same time had to present all the facts of the case. From the beginning the nation had been rebellious. Whether the "first father" was Abraham or Jacob, he failed to follow God's will but transgressed and caused problems for future generations. Likewise, many of those who interpreted the requirements of God, led the people astray. The "princes of the sanctuary," as the prophet called them (v. 28), would have their privileges removed. Not only would the religious leaders be stripped of their offices, robes, and honors, the entire nation would be reduced to a common level of reproach. This entire section seems aimed at making the people examine themselves and see that they contain no righteousness by which to claim merit. The prophet, like Paul much later, was determined to give the people, especially those who claimed to be religious, no grounds for having confidence in their own righteousness. If they were to be saved, like sinners in any generation, it must have been through God's free and unmerited love and mercy. As this part of the message concludes, the picture was gloomy. Israel was about to be destroyed. The "ban" or a "thorough devotion to destruction" is her fate. No longer would she be the light of the world. She had forfeited her rights as a chosen people. Only God's grace could save her. How true of us all!

V. Sufficiency (44:1-5)

The problem which constantly confronts the interpreter of this larger section is whether we have one extended discourse delivered upon a historical occasion or a series of smaller isolated messages which were placed side by side in the prophetic roll to constitute a literary unit. The sudden transition at this point intensifies the perplexity. As severely as he had condemned the nation and threatened destruction, the prophet consoled and promised to bless in an almost unprecedented way. The severity and gloom of the previous pronouncements are mitigated by a promise of future happiness. Like a refreshing rain, future generations would awaken to a full comprehension of the honor and dignity which comes to those who belong to God in a unique way.

Though the terms "Israel," "Jacob," and "chosen" have already been used, they are no less profoundly beautiful in this context. Nowhere do we see God's grace set forth more clearly than in these verses. One would, at first, think God had come to a full stop in dealing with Israel and had written her off as His covenant partner. Once more, however, He took up the theme of His purpose as though the "extirpation order" were an hindrance to his plan. Though we have a contrast, no break occurs between chapters 43 and 44. Having emphasized that Israel was a sinful nation from the start, the prophet stated the other side of the truth. Israel was chosen from the beginning to be God's servant, formed in the womb to be the agent of His redemptive program.

Israel Within Israel

Who is the servant? Ideally, of course, God chose the nation. In a real sense, however, God's servant is that portion of Israel that will respond to His will and seek to fulfill His purpose. As the prophetic symphony moves along, we shall gradually see that the entire nation would not allow herself to be a servant. Somewhere along the way, the concept changes to "Israel within Israel," perhaps at this point, and surely by a later statement, "Thou art my servant; Israel, in whom I will be glorified" (49:3). That which another spokesman for God said of his own calling (Jer. 1:4), the prophet here said of Israel as God's "prophet-people." The Lord knew both from the womb. God's choice of Israel resembled Jeremiah's calling and preparation as a prophet. The figure of servant predominates, but often it is combined with that of a priest or of the king who rules for God.

In only three other places does an Old Testament writer use the word *Jeshurun* for Israel (Deut. 32:15; 33:5,26). This poetical term comes from a root which means "upright" and probably suggests Israel under her ideal character in light of what God saw she could and might yet be. The prophet probably drew this term from the ancient poetical dramas of his nation's history and wished to make it clear that Israel would not be dismissed as a failure. The term *Jeshurun* is probably built linguistically like the tribal name *Zebulun* and represents an endearing diminutive. This would explain the Greek translator's rendering it "beloved." God still held His people in highest esteem and refused to cast them aside from the purpose for which He had called them.

A Twofold Symbolism

The double figure of "pour water" and "pour my Spirit" speaks of the regeneration, fertility and freshness, both physical and moral, that God would bring to the nation. Even as the New Testament would later say that God "will supply every need according to his abundance in Christ Jesus" (Phil. 4:19), so the God of Israel would be a source of sustenance for the returning exiles. He would minister to their whole person and bring victory out of what seemed at that time to be utter defeat. God's

Spirit would do this work. The very life of God would enter into the corpse, Israel, as she lay in her Tigris-Euphrates grave. God's original promise to Abraham was in the form of a blessing whose power would enable his seed to multiply and become as the stars of the sky for number. Though this seed had fallen upon the ground and seemingly died, the promise had not died. As another prophet was told that the dry bones would live (Ezekiel 37:5), so this prophet was told that "I will pour my Spirit upon thy seed, and my blessing upon thine offspring; and they shall spring up among the grass, as willows by the watercourses" (44:3-4).

From Horror to Hope

Concluding and climaxing this section, the prophet pictured the expanded kingdom of God. As God's people once again flourished prosperously, various ones would proclaim publicly that they belonged to Him. The threefold use of "this" to indicate the various groups in verse 5 suggests the turning would be of individuals rather than a mass movement. The rising generations who would proudly proclaim their association with Israel's God were, no doubt, both physical Israelites and people from heathen nations also. The name *Israel* would be all sufficient for it would represent the most honored and dignified designation possible, far surpassing all other titles. The prophet has passed from a message of horror to one of hope. He made plain the possibility of transformation, both physical and spiritual through God's grace. He who is Jacob may become an Israel, but he who is neither can become a member of God's family for His people are limited not by race or background but only by whether or not they will surrender in loving obedience to His will. The prophet would have agreed with John Oxenham who, centuries later, wrote that in God's kingdom through Christ, there is no east, west, south, or north because it is a "fellowship of love throughout the whole wide earth."

VI. Sarcasm (44:6-20)

To give authority to His statement concerning Israel's future, God, through His prophet, once more asserted His claim of complete superiority. No one even belongs in the same category with Him. In this section, the prophet stressed God's incomparable power and mocked at the idols workmen had created and worshiped as though they were gods. The vanities and absurdities accompanying such an approach to life were held up before the people with such sarcasm that one feels the prophet must have spoken with a sardonic smile as he delivered the message. After piling up divine names, the prophet emphasized the eternity of God as well as His uniqueness. Who else had ordered the course of history and understood from the beginning the issues and destiny of the human race? How can one possibly doubt when he views the works of God and His hand guiding all things according to His will and purpose?

Though some expositors feel verses 6 through 8 belong more properly with the previous unit as a sealing of God's promise to Israel, the best approach seems to recognize them as a prelude to the humorous rebuke of idolatry and the caricature the prophet draws of a person making his own tangible representation of a god and then worshiping it. Actually, the small section can be viewed as an ideal transition which would go well with either group of verses if the other did not exist. They are needed, however, to set the stage for the irony which follows.

Power and Values?

What is the existential mystique of idolatry? In the ancient world, each king believed his god went with him to war. Thus, if a nation was conquered, the implication was that the god had been conquered. Since the Jews had suffered defeat and Exile, the temptation was for them to believe the gods of the Babylonians were stronger than Yahweh. Yet, their prophet told them to trust in the God of Israel and refuse to forfeit their faith by turning to gods made with hands. As the Lord's representative, he of course saw an ethical reason for the Exile. The people had sinned against the moral requirements of their God. However, the divine spokesman promised redemption—deliverance from Babylon and restoration to their homeland. Having plead with forensic logic, the prophet next sought to illustrate the folly of idol worship by showing the process by which a false god came into being.

Underlying all of this logic was a spiritual dynamic regarding intangible power. When a person erects a substitute for the unseen God, he shows distrust of spiritual law and the ability of such a Deity to provide for his needs and help him in times of crisis. Idolaters, rather than trust in moral values, erect a tangible representation of an earthly desire and then pour out their allegiance to that craving by worshiping its concrete expression. Actually, we today have not gone far beyond this. Rather than erect a visible god, we worship the materialistic concept by indulging in the activities related to it. Where an atheistic leader says that religion is "the opiate of the people," Christians, if they understand the concept thoroughly, can reply, "Not in today's world. The true opiate of the people is commercialized entertainment and the sensual thrills that come from a thoroughly secular way of life." Idleness is another form of idolness!

Making and Worshipping an Idol

Notice the steps the prophet outlined in the manufacture of an idol! The fashioner sharpens a tool, takes a piece of metal, and works with it over a fire. He pounds it into shape with a hammer, laboring so intensely that he becomes hungry and thirsty. Next, the carpenter comes on the scene, measuring the wood, outlining a figure with chalk, and carving it out with his tools to make a handsome human figure that he can place in his house. Various types of wood might be used—cedars, oaks, or cypress. He might even plant a laurel tree and wait for the rain to make it grow.

Next, comes the real sarcasm! The prophet told how a man used some of a tree for fuel and some for the idol (vv. 15). He built a fire with part of the wood in order to keep himself warm and also to bake bread. The other part he made into a god and worshiped. Verses 16 and 17 seem to be a recapitulation, for effect, of verse 15. Perhaps the most striking statement in the entire section is, "and the residue thereof he maketh into a god" which led one preacher to deliver a message entitled "A God from the Leftovers."

What a commentary on modern-day Christianity! A writer illustrates the truth of this passage graphically: On a rainy Sunday afternoon, a little boy and girl, brother and sister, were playing Noah and the Ark. A shoe box was the ark, and the bathtub, the flood. When the flood was over, they decided to make a burnt offering to God. After arguing as to whose toy animal they would use, the little boy solved the problem. He ran to the attic and brought back a toy lamb, dirty, head smashed, and tail missing. "Here, let's give this to God. We will never want to use it again!" A god from the leftovers!

The Folly of It All!

Having described the process, the prophet turned to direct accusation. A person who manufactures his own god is stupid! His intellectual level is so low he is incapable of applying the most rudimentary principles of logic to his conduct. What he does makes about as much sense as eating ashes! He is so much a victim of his foolish ideas as to be beyond help. He is intellectually deficient, morally confused, and spiritually dead. He is not only blind to ethical values but is blind to the fact that he is blind. One translation says that his own deluded mind has misled him, and he cannot recollect himself so far as to say, "Why! this thing in my hand is a sham."

VII. Summary (44:21-28)

Like a modern-day evangelistic preacher preparing to give an invitation for public commitment, the prophet "pulled the strings together" as he concluded his message. Remember these things! He began to recite what he had already told them. God formed Israel. Then, He chose her to be His servant, redeemed her, and blotted out her transgressions. God was reminding Israel of the special relationship that existed between them and how this had resulted in the promise that the nation would be delivered from her sufferings. The series of magnificent utterances in this section expresses the nature and purpose of God in a way unsurpassed, perhaps unequaled, anywhere else in the Old Testament. God of creation united with God in history! An amazing and overwhelming combination!

Nature and Redemption

Since all nature is bound up with the history of humankind, the curse affects it so that it groans and travails in pain even as persons suffer for their sins. Likewise, nature rejoices because it profits when persons are redeemed. The classical example of this truth is found in Paul's words, "For the creation waits with eager longing for the revealing of the sons of God, . . . because the creation itself will be set free from its bondage to decay and obtain the glorious liberty of the children of God" (Rom. 8:19,21 RSV). The prophet, therefore, called upon every part of the universe, as he knew it, to burst into song. Not only the heavens, but the lower parts of the earth—Sheol—the place of departed spirits, were summoned to the rejoicing. Mountains and trees of the forest were to give their witness of the saving and redeeming grace of God. More wonderful than original creation would be the new creation!

God Acts in History!

A final prophetic thrust clinches the case! In the concluding section (vv. 24-28), the prophet used twelve participles to make his message graphic. All of his statements led to the final dramatic announcement which would introduce the new stage in the development of his theme. God had called Cyrus to accomplish His work! This was not actually a new thought, but, from now on, Cyrus and his political policies will be used as a preparation for understanding the unique Servant who would bring spiritual deliverance to the people of God.

Look at what the Lord has done! He is the one redeeming, forming, making all things, stretching out the heavens, hammering out the floor of the earth, frustrating the impostors, making fools of the diviners, refuting the wise men, confirming the word of His servant, saying that Jerusalem will once more be inhabited, commanding the deep waters to dry up, and proclaiming that Cyrus is His shepherd. What an impressive array of "action words," reflected by the participles, to convince the people that God has His hand on historical events.

To doubt One of such power would be sheer folly. A modern-day Christian says forcefully, "I am convinced that the culmination of all our experiences, the conclusion of all our failures, the sum of all our depressions, the final product of all our problems will bring us squarely up to the significant fact of God." Have faith in God! He cannot fail! He must prevail! Those who trust Him and live in the light of that commitment will prevail also!

5
Even a Fool Can Be a Tool
(45:1-25)

The title of this chapter does not suggest by any means that Cyrus the Great was deficient either intellectually or morally. Rather, I wish to stress as strongly as possible that God can use anyone, anywhere, anytime, to accomplish His purpose in history regardless of that person's mental ability or ethical insight. Scholars disagree on many things about the private life of Cyrus, but the Bible is uncompromising. God brought Cyrus on the scene for one purpose, to help work out the divine plan for worldwide redemption. Ask Greek historians such as Herodotus or Xenophon about Cyrus, and they would have replied that he was the ideal ruler. Such writers were not so concerned with what he did as what they thought he was. His simplicity, purity, wisdom, health, generosity, and what they called his moral influence—all served to make him attractive. They felt one could not emphasize his good qualities or his virtues too much in order that Cyrus may serve as an example for generations to come. However, bring him out of the light of these hero worshipers who have ignored reality in order to preach example, and let the austere faith judge him. Immediately, his brilliance is quenched and his character becomes neutral.

To Each His Own

Of course, each person operates from his own world view. If Herodotus had been asked to judge the Hebrew prophet's evaluation of Cyrus, he would have probably replied, "You claim Cyrus was raised up to let a few petty Jewish provincials return to their own corner of the earth. Foolish! I refuse to identify him with such sectarian interests. He was meant as a noble example for all mankind." The prophet knew better! He was convinced that, though the world always needs heroes to serve as examples, something greater must be given to it. Only redemption can meet humankind's need, and Israel had been chosen of God to bring the One into the world who would liberate all the peoples of the world from spiritual bondage.

Many sermons have come from this account of Cyrus. For years, theological students have been pointed to Parker's "Every Life a Plan of God" as an excellent example of presenting a relevant truth from an ancient source. In more recent days, Fosdick's "The Impossibility of Being Irreligious" has emphasized the fact that every person, whether he realizes it or not, fits into the divine scheme of things.

God Works in Strange Ways

How true! God guides the disobedient, the secular, sometimes even the atheistic world to perform actions that advance His kingdom. For instance, Joseph's brothers sold him into slavery, but this made possible for the tribes to be spared from a famine and assured their existence. An Egyptian princess found a small baby in an ark and used her royal prerogative to take him as her own. God used this—in a sense—selfish deed years later to deliver a slave people and thus redemption was born. Caesar Augustus sent out a decree that uprooted many people and sent them on trips that probably most could not afford. Because of this greed-motivated act, however, Jesus was born in Bethlehem where prophecy said the event would take place. Pontius Pilate played the coward and allowed the mob to put Jesus on the cross not knowing the deed was done by the "determinate counsel and foreknowledge of God." In these, and many other cruel and capricious choices, a divine purpose is hidden away in the heart of the happenings. A guiding hand works that becomes clear only as time reveals and vindicates God's hand and purpose in history. A contemporary historian would have found it impossible to believe that of all the royal decrees sent forth by Cyrus when he conquered Babylon the most important and far reaching was the one that allowed less than a hundred-thousand captive people to return to their poverty-stricken home and rebuild their burnt-down house of worship! Wisdom, however, is justified of her children! Let us examine further this seemingly small event that had such cosmic proportions and implications!

I. Decree (45:1-8)

Though the actual words of the Lord seem to begin with the second verse, they are mingled with the prophet's description in the first. This mode of composition is often in the Hebrew text because the writers thought more of an idea than the form in which it was expressed. The accumulation of descriptive phrases probably comes from the fact that the prophet's one main object was to impress upon the reader's mind the attributes of God and, therefore, those of His chosen instrument. Earlier the Lord called Cyrus "my shepherd" (44:28), but here He went even further. The term *anointed* continues the emphasis on a close personal relationship between Cyrus and Israel's God. This word is used in several ways by Old Testament writers. Prophets, priests, and kings were all set apart by an anointing from the Lord. The Messianic Redeemer, at least twice (Ps. 2:7; Dan. 9:25 *ff.*), is designated by this term. The normal sequel is that the Spirit of God rests upon the one who is anointed for special service. We should, of course, understand that this solemn appointment of Cyrus meant only that God had set him apart for an important public service in His cause. In no way did the prophet imply that Cyrus was a man of piety or a worshiper of the true God. This title does not designate holiness of character but assignment to an office.

Work of Cyrus

The phrase "whose right hand I have holden" suggests that God had sustained and strengthened Cyrus as we do when we take by the hand one who is feeble. Indeed, Cyrus did "subdue nations" as indicated by Xenophon who described his empire as "extending from the Mediterranean and Egypt to the Indian Ocean and from Ethiopia to the Euxine Sea." Also, he described its extent by observing that "the extremities were difficult to inhabit, from opposite causes—some from excess of heat, and others from excess of cold; some from a scarity of water, and others from too great abundance." What a conquerer! The prophet, however, gave God the credit, not Cyrus.

The phrase that says God will "loose the loins of kings" refers to the dress of that day. The people wore large, flowing robes thrown over an undergarment or tunic which was shaped to the body. The outer robe was girded with a sash which held the robe down when they worked, ran, or went to war. One "girded up his loins" when he prepared for toil and to "unloose the girdle" meant to make it difficult, if not impossible, to perform in strenuous activity such as fighting. The phrases "open the doors before him" and "gates shall not be shut" most likely referred specifically to the conquest of Babylon. Herodotus said there were one-hundred gates in the walls that surrounded the city of Babylon. In addition, there were walls within on each side of the Euphrates, the river which ran through the city. The inhabitants had access to the river and, even more important, any invader who penetrated the outer walls would still face the task of coming in through the inner gates. Usually, these gates were, of course, closed, but on the night Belshazzar was slain and Cyrus entered the city, the gates were open. If these gates had remained closed as was the custom, the Persians would have been shut in the bed of the river and all of them could have been easily destroyed. The palace gates were also left open because of the revelry that night. Every part of the city was thus available for conquest and plunder. How marvelously exact were the prophet's words concerning the historical situation!

Why God Did It

God determined to take away everything that might in any way retard or oppose the victorious march of Cyrus. The references in verse 2 to making the rough places smooth, breaking the doors of brass, and cutting the bars of iron suggest that serious obstacles would disappear before the Lord's powerful resources. These gates or doors were most likely those of the outside walls while the gates in verse 1 were the "two-leaved gates" around the Euphrates. The "treasures of darkness" and "hidden riches of secret places" refer to the wealth that kings had in obscure and strong places, not to be touched except in an emergency. Fabulous stories have been told about the wealth of Croesus, king of Lydia, and how Cyrus seized it when he captured the city. Babylon also was reputed to have as much or even more stored in unsuspected places.

A threefold purpose caused God to do His marvelous work of equipping Cyrus for the task. The same Hebrew phrase precedes each of them although the second time it is translated differently from the first and the third. First, God would do all of this "that thou mayest know" (45:3)—that Cyrus might be aware—it was Israel's God who was making him strong for his task. The second is rendered "For Jacob my servant's sake" (45:4) while the third is "that they may know from the rising of the sun, and from the west, that there is none beside me" (45:6). The final is of course the climax and represents the ultimate purpose of God. He desires that all people everywhere in the world shall come to a knowledge of Him. For this purpose, He called Abraham and, though the promise would not be realized completely until Jesus came, and then of course not literally, God always held this as an ideal in every statement concerning His redemptive program.

Everything Comes From God

The statement "I form the night, and create darkness" (v. 7) is considered by some as an attack upon Zoroastrian dualism with its antagonism between Ahuramazda, the god of light and goodness, and Ahriman, the god of darkness and evil. Most modern scholars, however, doubt the prophet had this in mind since we do not know that Cyrus was familiar with this concept. In fact, the evidence indicates the Persian general preceded the religious leader. The "I make peace and create evil" does not solve the age-old question of who started wickedness in the first place. Human choice did that in the Garden of Eden. Rather, the "evil" is the physical punishment that comes upon persons in the law of sin and retribution. God originated this law, but we cannot blame Him with deliberate and capricious creation of sinfulness. The "peace" is more than the absence of war or trouble. Perhaps the expressions *well being* or *wholeness* best translate the Hebrew word. The Qumran scroll reads "good" in the place of "peace" and this is of course the opposite of evil. The basic thrust of the prophet in this particular segment seemed to be that God refused to be identified with any of the polytheistic systems. He is the sole Creator. All things and people come from Him and are eventually responsible to Him, even Cyrus.

A Lyrical Outburst

A true genius knows how to relieve the tension in a drama or the excitement of profound thought by the unexpected insertion of light relief. Verse 8 represents such an input, a brief poem, but one containing a great declaration of faith. This lyrical outburst deals with the happy state that will follow the liberation of Israel by Cyrus and the reign of righteousness and salvation that will be established. The word *righteousness* is a favorite of the prophet, but he did not always use it with exactly the same thrust. Here it is almost a synonym for *salvation* although it does retain some of the idea of God's moral and ethical demands for holy living as the divine will for mankind. Perhaps we might best understand it as combined with deliverance, the basic idea of salvation, to picture the order that will prevail in the world when God's will is sovereign. This will be a happy time, and the very elements of nature will participate in the rejoicing.

The figure of rain and dew descending from heaven and watering the earth, producing beauty and fertility, suggests the piety and peace that would be present when the people were liberated and took their place once more in Jerusalem, their home. During the captivity, they had been away from their land and Temple. The praises of God had ceased, and the situation was strikingly similar to the earth when rain is withheld. Better days were coming! Once more the altars would burn with sacrifices and God's glory would go forth from His house! The prophet saw even more! He visualized the distant days when the Messiah would come and God's redemptive message would go forth to the nations. Both short-range and long-term pictures are always included in the prophetic message!

II. Defense (45:9-13)

The skeptics we have with us always! When the prophet told how God had chosen Cyrus to implement His will, many were slow to believe this good news. How impatient he became with them we do not know, but this section of his message indicates he had sharp words, especially for those who questioned the propriety of God's selecting Cyrus rather than a descendant of David as the liberator of Israel. Perhaps a division arose among the people with some partially accepting his message and others rejecting it outright. Though we do not know enough about the complaint, we can sense the strong feeling of the prophet.

Who has a right to criticize God? Is He not the One who brought us into being, and are we not dependent upon Him for every benefit we enjoy? Those who were complaining insisted on believing only what they could see with their eyes, but the prophet viewed the seemingly hopeless situation with reckless faith, believing that the One who shaped the clay had a purpose in mind and would not cease until He made it a reality in history. Woe to those who as complaining children find fault with the One who is working with perfect knowledge and an abundant of resources!

Let God Be God

Bold figures of speech invigorate the message. Do scraps of clay have a right to direct the One moulding them! Only a wicked and foolish son would complain to his father about the circumstances of his birth. Who would dream of telling a woman in labor what kind of child she should bring into the world! Let the Creator be the Creator! The prophet blasted the opposition for attacking the divine plan. Such an approach represented not only a lack of faith but a lack of respect. Rebellion caused them to act in this way, and such an attitude represented a form of spiritual suicide.

Not that God refused to be examined! He welcomed open inquiry if done in a proper way and with a reverent recognition of His sovereignty. Only the insecure refuse to explain their actions. The people, however, must have recognized certain facts about their God. For one thing, he is the Creator. Three times in verses 12 and 13 the personal pronoun is used seperately for emphasis as God said plainly, "I have made the earth . . . I . . . stretched out the heavens . . . I have . . . raised up Cyrus." God, and no one else, caused these things to happen. From His self-sufficiency, He did that which pleased Him and that which was necessary to His redemptive program in the world.

What about Cyrus? The same God who chose Israel ruled with sovereignty over this Persian king. He called Cyrus for a divine purpose even as He did Israel. The difference is He chose Cyrus to be a saving instrument for Israel who would, in turn, produce the Savior for the world. Which of the exiles, unless enlightened by God's Spirit, would ever have been able to figure that out! The two parallel lines, Israel and Cyrus, converged not in infinity but at a particular moment in time and at a specific spot on earth. This intersecting of God's two servants occured in 536 BC when Cyrus, two years after he conquered Babylon, decreed the Jewish captives who so desired could go home and rebuild their city and Temple.

The "not for price nor reward" (v. 13) means the miracle of history occured without the Gentile ruler even knowing he was a part of the divine plan for world redemption. Whether or not Cyrus, even in a limited way, became a believer in Israel's God is an interesting subject for speculation but is not relevant at this point. The use of "anointed" (v. 1) to describe Cyrus gives a "warm feeling" toward him. God, through the mouth of Jeremiah, called Nebuchadnezzar "my servant" (25:9), but this designation of Cyrus is even stronger. The air of mystery that is thrown around Cyrus fascinates us, but we should give the glory to God not to the Persian king. That monarch, partially enlightened though he may have been, knew nothing of the significance of his work. He was a tool in the hand of Israel's God. Though he was probably better in character than Nebuchadnezzar and certainly more moral than Sennacherib, he was nevertheless only a tool. All things are in the hand of God!

III. Delights (45:14-17)

Though Israel did not yet understand the dynamics of God's doings, she was nevertheless in for some great days! Favors would be conferred upon her in spite of her disobedience. Since Egypt, Ethiopia, and the Sabeans were mentioned earlier (43:3) as the ransom God gave to Persia for release of Israel, some scholars feel the prophet meant these nations would come over to Cyrus, becoming his slaves and bowing down as was the custom at later Roman triumphs. The context, as well as the literary structure—the feminine pronoun occurring five times in this one verse—make it clear "thee" must refer to Jerusalem, the mother of Israel and thus symbolizing the nation.

The Self-Hidden God

In what sense did these nations become slaves to Israel or surrender their loyalty to this small handful of exiles who were about to return home? Though couched in a material framework, the message is much deeper. Physical treasure is of course desirable, but spiritual wealth supersedes it. The ultimate fulfillment of passages such as these is found in the messianic Kingdom which was brought into the world through Jesus Christ. No doubt many became monotheists because God blessed Israel, but even this is not the true meaning of the passage. The "in chains" does not mean Israel would put physical bonds upon them but rather symbolizes the future Lordship of Christ over all who receive Him as their Savior, becoming, like Paul, a bondslave of Jesus Christ (Rom. 1:1). Did the people of that day understand it? Of course, not! Even today, some still consider such passages as not yet fulfilled predictions of material wealth for national Israel. Verse 15 poses a problem in interpretation for some who feel the phrase "thou art a God who hidest thyself" was spoken by the converted heathen to their previously worshiped idols, accusing them of being gods that could not interpret history or bring deliverance. More likely, however, these words were addressed to the true God, the Holy One of Israel, as an apostrophe by the prophet. Overcome with the majesty of the message God had proclaimed, the prophet burst into ecstatic comment about the greatness of his God.

Does God actually hide Himself or was this figure of speech, a provocative turning of the phrase to attract attention and put across a spiritual point the prophet felt needed to be made? Some ranges of color and sound are so made that our senses are not capable of receiving them. The ether is full of waves and oscillations which are physiologically beyond our comprehension. Likewise, spiritual truth is available and understood only by those who are conditioned for it. The glory of a victory is always in the striving for it.

The spiritual world refuses to give its deeper truths to the casual passerby or the superficial visitor who has only a passing interest. The secret of attaining spiritual truth is to hunger and thirst after it. If, without any deep desire for or striving after a vision of God on our part, He suddenly appeared and made Himself known, life would make no demand on our character or require any commitment to truth. God hides Himself in order to challenge us. He must preserve our moral initiative and, most of all, our individuality. A wise parent will not work out a problem for a child but rather teach the child how to work it out for himself. One wise man once said that if God were to offer in one hand the immutable truth, and in the other the search, he would say in all humility, "Lord, keep the absolute truth for it is not suited to me. Leave to me only the power and the desire to seek for it, though I never wholly find it." Praise God that He hides Himself in order that we might have the privilege of seeking Him out!

The Revealed God

On the other hand, some things must be revealed! Unless the prophet, inspired of God, had pointed out the mystery of God's grace in calling Cyrus, the people never would have "figured it out" for themselves. Revelation means that God takes the first step in making Himself known. God hides Himself when it is necessary but manifests Himself when the time is right. In His self-emptying, God is most truly present. Let this mind be in you which was also in Christ Jesus!

How arrogant the unregenerate world considers a person who claims to have a knowledge of God not possessed by everyone! The powerful pagan people must have considered it an insult to their craftiness to be told that, apart from the God of Israel, they would be confounded and ashamed in the day of crisis. Likewise, the contemporary world feels self-sufficient and resents the Christian community insisting that God is hidden from persons until He is revealed in Jesus Christ. What spiritual arrogance! "I simply can't understand you Christians saying a person is lost without Jesus and never saved until he comes in repentance and faith to one who lived and died nearly two-thousand years ago" says the modern sophisticate. The Christian agrees completely. He does not understand it. No one understands how lost he is until that person is delivered from his own darkness. Only one who has seen the world in the light of God's revelation understands how deep the darkness is outside of Jesus Christ. Only one who has been reconciled to God by the Savior's love realizes how alienated he was before the experience took place.

Many delightful experiences were in store for Israel. The true redemption, however, was not in national Israel but the spiritual nucleus who would be usable in God's plan. The final realization of the promise will be the everlasting salvation of those who call upon the name of Jesus Christ, the highest revelation of God. Only these will "not be put to shame nor confounded" or know a salvation that is "world without end" (vv. 17). Another inspired man of God said, "Take delight in the Lord and he will give you the desires of your heart" (Ps. 37:4, RSV). The prophet agreed in essence with a slightly different thrust, "Desire the Lord with all thy heart, and he will give you the things that delight."

IV. Demand (45:18-25)

One final word remains, an invitation or perhaps better, a command to the escapees, but first the prophet reaffirmed that God is the sole Power of the world. No new thought, of course, but one he felt necessary at this place in his message. Three key words used in the Genesis origin account—*created, made,* and *formed*—are also used by the prophet in this context as he called the people to unwavering confidence in the true God. He set forth in strong language the divine intent in bringing the world into existence. God did not create it for confusion but as a place in which people could live with both peace and purpose. The inference is certainly present that since God had made all the world for habitation, He certainly wanted the land of Judah, which He had chosen as a special place, to once more become a populated area. Some scholars have gone so far as to see in this statement a suggestion, if not an actual promise, implicit though it may be at this point, that this earth shall be inhabited after the resurrection. One scholar contends strongly that there are "fewer reasons why the earth shall be inhabited *then* than there are now; nor can there be any reasons why the earth should *then* exist in vain any more than now." However one feels about this suggestion, the prophet's basic contention was clear and on that he would not compromise. One God! One purpose! One way of finding fulfillment! All other claims to deity are false!

God Reveals as He Wishes

God has always been open, making Himself and His will known revealingly! The phrase "have not spoken in secret" (v. 19) does not contradict the prophet's previous statement "thou art a God that hidest thyself" (45:15) though the same Hebrew word is used. Any doctrine of revelation has one assumption. God is unknown and unknowable except as He chooses to manifest Himself to His creation. Even on a human level, close associates never penetrate to the innermost recesses of each other's personality. The prophet means God does not hide Himself with dubious oracles and thus force the people to consult the magical arts or the devious practices of sorcery and superstition. God's method of revealing Himself stands in sharp contrast with the dark practices of the heathen soothsayers.

When God called upon His people to serve Him through the years, it was not His plan for them to go unrewarded. Those who follow God realize inexpressibly great and valuable benefits. In times of trial, persecution, and affliction, God had brought them encouragement both through His prophetic word and His salvation acts in history. When He invited the Israelites to seek Him, He purposed from the beginning to respond to their prayers. Rather than being a God who ignores, He is One who vindicates. He speaks righteousness and effects the proclamation of things that are right. All of the evils that follow the practice of sorcery are repugnant to the Holy One of Israel. Nothing that he commanded was unprofitable. This could not be said about the false gods who approved and recommended nothing. God always gave direct answers in contrast to the ambiguous and deceitful responses of those who manipulated the idols. God's Word, since it is alive, is compelled by its very nature to express itself through an explosive situation—in living form. God did indeed become visible and knowable when He climaxed His revelation centuries later by sending His Son into the world who, in the days of His flesh, said, "I have spoken openly to the world; I ever taught in synagogues and in the temple, where all the Jews come together; and in secret spake I nothing" (John 18:20).

A Demanding Invitation

Having set the stage with a firm statement concerning Himself, God was now ready to give the invitation which should more properly be considered a command since three imperatives were used to express it. Scholars are not in full agreement concerning the audience to whom the demand was given. The prophet certainly had the Jews in mind, but the language suggests very strongly that he referred to both the Israelites and the heathen who had escaped the judgment that fell upon the world in the wars accompanying the overthrow of the nations as Cyrus became master of the international scene. Since unfaithful Jews as well as the heathen practiced idolatry, the command to "assemble yourselves and come; draw near together" applies to both groups (v. 20). The phrase "They . . . that carry the wood of their graven image" probably refers to the annual new year festival in Babylon when the worshipers bore their gods in procession through the streets. Perhaps it refers to the fact that the people had to carry their gods into battle with them though they sought aid from them. The conclusion is obvious. They were gods that could neither protect nor deliver!

Though the imperatives "declare" and "bring forth" have no objects, the general verdict of expositors is that the prophet was issuing a command for the escaped to set forth their cause if they felt they had one. These verbs are followed by an imperfect in the third person rather than the second, but it still has the idea of "let them" which is at least a mild imperative. Perhaps, as some contend, the third person suggests the people were unwilling to accept the challenge or were at least in doubt about it, and the prophet invited them to deliberate together or at least seek the advice of someone who knew more than they did about spiritual things.

Refusing to wait upon the people, however, the Lord stated His case.

He only had foretold what would happen. Who else had been able to interpret history so eloquently and accurately? Israel's God had proved again and again that He alone is alive and full of creative goodness. No one else was competent to speak with such authoritative righteousness for He only is unqualified holiness! No one else was so merciful, delivering people from their sin solely by His grace. Since no one else combined these two attributes, Israel's God stood alone, august and unique!

No One Like Israel's God

Now comes the invitation! Though it may not seem as warmhearted as the plea of Jesus to "Come unto me, all ye that labor and are heavy laden, and I will give you rest" (Matt. 11:28), the thought as well as the literary structure is strikingly similar. Before the Savior issued His invitation, He made a stupendous statement concerning His own person and His relationship with the Father. In this context also, the prophet said in essence that God is both just and Justifier, a righteous God and a Saviour in one Person. No other deity in the history of religion has ever combined these two traits. Included in this loving invitation is the desire and eager longing for "all the ends of the earth" (v. 22) to share this marvelous gift of God's grace. An impressive fact about this larger section is how the balance is preserved in the prophetic concern for both Israel and the nations. Each time God presented a bright prospect for Israel, He expanded it to include the remainder of mankind. When properly understood, the Old Testament, especially the Prophets, represents a universal concern of God equal to the New Testament.

In order to give the most solemn assurance possible that His purpose in history would be implemented, God swore by Himself (v. 23) This means He affirmed solemnly that the event was as certain to occur as that God exists. A parallel expression is "As I live" which occurs often in the Old Testament. In fact, Paul quoted this passage and used the phrase "as I live" as equivalent to the prophet's words (Rom. 14:11). God's oath preceded a word of universal hope. Many early theologians saw "a clear promise from the lips of the living God expressed in living words." These scholars reasoned that, like arrows shot from the bow, the words must hit their target because God Almighty had sent forth and His message must abide forever. How can a statement fail if spoken by One who possesses all resources for making it become a reality!

Paul's eloquent statement to the Philippians has made the prophet's "every knee shall bow, every tongue shall swear" a household phrase for every Christian theologian. Is this teaching universalism—that every person will be saved? Does it mean that a time will come on earth when, through the preaching of the gospel, everyone will become a Christian? Not at all! Though some scholars insist this verse was fulfilled existentially when Jesus conquered death and arose victoriously, such a concept is too much in the ethereal to be a practical teaching. The phrase will have its ultimate fulfillment eschatologically. John told us that when Christ shall come in the clouds "every eye will see him, every one who pierced him; and all the tribes of the earth will wail on account of him" (Rev. 1:7 RSV). When history is consummated, even those who opposed God's revelation vociferously and violently will be forced to acknowledge both His sovereignty and His righteousness, though it will be too late for their personal salvation.

The moving song of praise "Victory in Jesus" could well have been inspired by the composer's reading the prophet's glowing testimony of the sufficiency which we all find in God's highest revelation of Himself (45:24). The word *strength* was added because the Hebrew term *righteousness,* more properly translated "victory" in this context, produces the resources that give one the ability to cope in any situation. When a person is assured he is properly related to God through the "imputed righteousness" of the Savior, he is "able unto all things" that may confront him. On the other hand, those who insist on opposing God and even go so far as to be "incensed" against Him shall not only go down in defeat but utter frustration. Nowhere in the New Testament is the gospel message so clearly presented in all of its promises and warnings! Substituting the word *Jesus* in verses 24 and 25 puts this passage on a par with anything ever written by John or Paul.

A New Testament Parallel

In what sense are we to interpret the prophet's word that all Israel shall "be justified and shall glory," the concluding and climactic statement in this message? As said above, the prophet nowhere ever stated or implied that every person would find personal salvation either in Old Testament days nor in the Christian era. The Hebrew-translated "all" has too many shades of meaning for us ever to insist on an entirely literal application in any context. We read, for instance, in one passage that "all" the Philistines were killed but several chapters later here come some more Philistines. Who were killed? All of those who were there at that particular time! A New Testament passage is similar. Paul wrote to a group of Christians (Rom. 11:26) that "so all Israel shall be saved." Does this mean that every Jew who ever lived will be miraculously delivered from sin though he rejected God's revelation in his day? Of course not! If our Jewish friends wait to call upon Jesus for personal salvation until He comes in the sky to deliver them from the armies who are threatening their land, it will be too late! What then? Both the prophetic passage and the Pauline passage seem to be parallel in that the emphasis is not on the "all" but on the phrase that precedes it. The prophet said that "In the Lord" (RSV) shall all the seed of Israel be justified. The apostle said that in this manner shall all Israel be saved. All who are saved will be saved in the way that God has set forth. Any interpretation that teaches a universal salvation denies and vitiates the clear teaching of the Scriptures that a person must personally decide for Jesus. God saves "retail" not "wholesale" and only when a person comes individually as a result of his own decision.

God Can Use Us

As we conclude and summarize, we should look back at the beginning. God has complete control of everything, including empires and world movements. He can use any instrument to bring about His purposes. Froude, the historian, said that "even the Turks were guardian angels to the infant Gospel." Every person who has been exposed to the gospel message has a choice. He can be a believer with a prophetic consciousness and dedication, serving God intelligently and volitionally or, if necessary, he can be a "Cyrus" whom God used though Cyrus "knew him not." To put it another way in the words of a contemporary Christian, "God is going on with his work: with us if he may, or without us if he must." The person who is wise will serve God willingly and know the full joy of dedication to Him who is both Creator and Redeemer!

6
Is Your Religion a Load or a Lift?
(46:1-13)

A weight or a wing? Burden or buoyance? Load or lift? What is your religious life? Do you remember the days when in our church life we stressed "programming" so much that the main concern was to make 100 percent attendance every Sunday? One minister recalls with a smile that a group in a Sunday School class discussed at length what "on time" meant, and they finally compromised by saying that if you were on the parking lot in time to hear the group singing the opening song in the assembly, you count yourself as on time and receive the 10 percent alloted on the record slip for that accomplishment. Another recalls a group that put on a special effort to have every member present and every member 100 percent on a given Sunday. Happily every member was present that day, but one man, an editor for the religious publishing house that produced their study literature, had some bad news. He said, "I have been travelling all week, came in late yesterday tired, and forgot to study my lesson. We can't be a 100 percent group." One member suggested, "Go over by yourself and read the lesson hurriedly. That will qualify you." He refused, on the grounds of ethical integrity, insisting this would not really be honest. Guess what? When they came to study the lesson, they found he was the author of the material in the denominational publishing house's literature for that Sunday. Could he legitimately count himself as studying the lesson? *No! He had not reread it the week leading up to that Sunday!* Shades of first-century pharisaism!

Value of Rules

Let it be said immediately that great benefits came from those days. We learned to "play by the rules" and discipline ourselves to touch all the bases. This is important. Do you remember the day Marv Throneberry, with the New York Yankees, hit a triple, with two out, to bring in the tying run from first? The shortstop threw the ball to second and Marv was out for not touching the bag. Yankees' manager Casey Stengle "threw a fit" but the umpire said, "Cool it, Casey. He didn't touch first either." Proper procedures, even in our religious life and worship, have their place and keep us from becoming complete "free wheelers" lacking any responsibility. Such an attitude is as dangerous to proper worship as pharisaism.

On the other hand, when we stress the forms of organized religion so much that we "wear ourselves out" performing the meticulous duties required by institutionalism our religious life becomes a "load" instead of a "lift." Churchgoing becomes something we *must* do instead of something we *wish* to do and indeed *find joy* in doing. To put it another way, we must carry our God instead of our God carrying us. Such an approach to worship and religion may on the surface seem sufficient in peaceful times when no problems confront us. When the crisis comes, however, we find ourselves totally inadequate to cope, and the ecclesiastical system neither gives us any answers nor provides any internal resources.

Against the background of Israel's rapidly approaching deliverance from Babylon, the prophet brought a short message, continuing one of the symphony's chief themes, idolatry and the foolishness demonstrated by anyone who gives allegiance to these "not gods" which are made by human hands. Old Testament scholars are virtually unanimous in considering chapter 46 as a separate unit which could be lifted from the material and considered as an independent pericope although it fits beautifully in the continuity of the prophet's unfolding poetical masterpiece. Though all expositors do not agree on an outline of the contents, three main thoughts stand out in the prophet's message. Verses 1 and 2 present the *consternation* facing the idolaters as they saw their gods threatened by the coming invader, packed them on the backs of their domestic animals, and led them out of the city to safety. Verses 3 through 7 give a *contrast* between Israel's God who is alive and watches over His people and those nonentities whom the foolish ones worshiped. Verses 8 through 13 present a *call* from the prophet to his fellow Israelites to remember what God had done in the past for them, to listen to His announcements concerning what He was about to do through Cyrus, and to repent of their wickedness as their salvation drew near.

I. Consternation (46:1-2)

Threat of invasion always causes panic in a city. People seize their most valued possessions and flee for safety. This segment of the symphonic drama was no doubt presented on the eve of Babylon's capture. With creative imagination, the prophet envisioned what would happen when that which was about to occur became reality. Either of two interpretations fit the context. One view says the conquerer follows the old custom of a triumphant warrior and carries off the defeated gods of his foes as trophies to his own "showcase." Another suggests the subdued inhabitants of Babylon pack up their own idols at his approach. Whichever school of thought we accept, confusion, chaos, and consternation prevailed in the metropolitan center which had stood for years as the political and cultural capital of the world.

Babylonian Deities

The dignity of the two imaginary deities shines forth in the text as we see the extent to which these names enter into the composition of men's names both in sacred and secular history. *Belshazzar, Belteshazzar, Belesys! Nebuchadnezzar, Nebuzaradan, Nabopolassar!* We need no more than these examples to help us understand passages where the names are simply used to represent the Babylonian gods collectively.

Each year the prophet had probably watched at the annual festival of Akitu as the procession of gods paraded through the streets on the way to the E-Sagila shrine. Marduk, the most important of them, was known also by the name of *Bel* which, like the Hebrew term *Baal,* was a generic term for any god. He was indeed the guardian god of the city while Nebo, who was worshiped most prolifically and intensely at Borsippa in a magnificent temple called E-Zida, was the son of Bel. His name is from the same Semitic root as the Hebrew *navi,* the word translated "prophet" and was generally known as the speaker of the gods, like Mercury to whom Paul was likened (Acts 14:12) because he was the chief speaker.

Humorous Sarcasm

No one, certainly not a foreigner elbowing his way by as the procession of gods passed, would have dared to make a sarcastic remark as did the prophet. This would have been religious heresy and political treason. Those among the Israelites who were old enough may have remembered, as they saw the numbness of the Babylonian gods, their own debacle fifty years earlier when Zion's hill became a heap of ruins. The prophet showed his sense of humor as he pictured those gods made by human hands nearly toppling as the cart carrying some of them hit a rut or cobblestone. Brimming with sarcasm to the gods' attendants as they stumbled and tried to rescue their precious load, the prophet in verse 2 reversed the order of the Hebrew verbs which he used for "tottering" gods and "stumbling" men. A ludricous thought struck him. In a previous message (45:23), he had spoken of every human knee bowing down to the one true God. Now, he uses the same verb of proud Bel, whom the Babylonians delighted to enthrone as king over all the earth, picturing him as bowing down when the one whom Israel's God had anointed to deliver His people stood at the gate of the city. Utter humiliation characterized the "king-god" as his fruitless efforts were evident to all his devotees.

When modern-day "human gods" fail us, we are left with nothing. Such is the fate of those who reject the spiritual and cling only to the material.

II. Contrast (46:3-7)

Though some interpreters feel verses 3 and 4 link more logically with the preceding section, they, when combined with the three following ones, actually form a distinct unit presenting a vivid picture of the difference between Israel's God and the idols whom the pagans and unfaithful Jews worshiped. The prophet presented this contrast to instruct the foolish Israelites who had begun to think the Babylonian gods were more powerful than their own. No real reason can be found for considering "house of Jacob" and "remnant of Israel" anything except two phrases for the same group of people. The latter describes them more specifically and points out that those in Babylonian Exile were indeed the "good figs" (Jer. 24:4-7), and the ones who would carry on God's redemptive purposes in distinction to those left in Judah.

With tenderness and endearment, the prophet likened the relation between God and Israel to that of mother and child. In most cases, a mother cares for her offspring from the womb and through the tender years of helplessness, but, when the child grows up, the mother sends her out on her own. God, however, had continued to extend His helping hand to Israel. This continuity of compassion served as a promise that the Lord would not forsake Israel even when the hairs turn gray. In verse

4, the prophet used the first-person pronoun separate from the verb which emphasizes the intensity of God's action and the certainty that what He has been to them in the past He will be for all time. *I am the same! I will carry! I have made! I will bear! I will carry! I will deliver!* A stative verb, followed by strong active ones! What was true of the past is true now and will be true of the future!

Of course, we should probably be charitable enough to charge the Israelites only with syncretism. Rather than completely giving up the worship of their God, they merely began to give allegiance to other gods also, believing the latter were more powerful at that time in history or at least in the country where Israel was, at present, living. Expediency in worship and religious loyalties is no new phenomenon but has been with us a long time! Twice before (40:18,25), the prophet had challenged the people with similar words, but he obviously felt this occasion was too good to let pass, and, as he saw Bel and Nebo brought from their hidden places in the gaudy palace and displayed publicly in the parade, he could not hold back his sarcasm. To compare anyone with the great "I Am" of the Hebrews was folly because the utter impossibility of anyone being in any way like Him was self-evident in light of Israel's history.

The prophet's satirical taunt continued as he once more pictured how the gods were manufactured. The verbs reveal the cynical sneer of the message. The word rendered "lavish" means to shake up and pour out, and the noun from this verb root is translated "glutton" when describing the disobedient son in the discourse of Moses shortly before the great lawgiver's death (Deut. 21:20). The idea is that of squandering, as the prophet suggested the people spared no expense in pouring out their gold, as though it were vile and worthless, to make themselves a god to whom they could give their allegiance. The statement that they "weighed" silver (v. 6) perhaps suggests that they used silver so profusely they did not even bother to count it as they did the grosser metals. They held back nothing as they assigned their wealth to a crude object that in their darkened minds they erroneously believed could meet their needs in a crisis.

Once the resources had been provided for the metal god, someone was needed to implement the procedure. Thus their god would be a "two-fold" man-made object: first, from their wealth; and then from the hands of a hired artisan. Every part of the prophet's message derided those who believed the work of their own ability could serve as their deliverer when they faced the straits of extremity.

Foolish People

Three times previously (40:19; 41:7; 44:9 *ff.*), the prophet has described the making of idols, but the verbs in this context represent perhaps the greatest sarcasm. Though some versions translate the first two verbs in verse 7 as passive, they are both active. The people lifted the gods up on their shoulders! They carried them! The emphasis is on the foolish actions of the people not on the fact that the gods were "carried." Though the gods were as dead and lifeless as the gold and other metals used in them, the people treated them as though they had life. Having lifted them up and borne them, they set them in their permanent place from which the gods could not even move if disaster arose. Neither could they answer the people when they called unto them. What a contrast to the ever-living God of Israel who, through the mouth of another prophet, said, "Call unto me, and I will answer thee, and will show thee great things, and difficult, which thou knowest not" (Jeremiah 33:3).

Two men with keen insights, one a minister and the other a statesman, gave pungent comments on this portion of the prophet's message. The first pointed out that we have a contrast here in burden bearing and activity but also in power. He said, "Worship that seemed sufficient in peaceful times had proved totally inadequate when the crisis came. That was the real lesson the Babylonians learned. Lip service to a god who was not real was absolutely useless when the chips were down." He then asked, "Are we not proving that today? This world . . . presents a terrifying picture, and the gods in which we place our trust are in fact threatening our destruction. I wonder if we who profess to be Christians are reaping the fruit of years of lip service to the Lord who has never been real to us, while the true worship of our heart has been given elsewhere." The nonclergy statesman agreed and carried the truth a bit further, "If we cannot fulfill our own ideals, we cannot expect others to accept them." Perhaps the problem is that we set up the ideal of a Christian society, but we do not attain it because our "god" is not real. He is merely a patron of the society instead of our sovereign Lord. God does not wish to be patronized. He demands that He be obeyed!

III. Call (46:8-13)

Hebrew prophecy contained one essential ingredient that set it apart
from the oracles of other religions that existed in its day. Though it began
within the context of contemporary events, it never stopped there. Before
the speaker concluded, he invited—even urged—the people to become
a part of God's larger purpose in the world. More often than not, he
pointed backward before he looked forward. The fact that God had
carried His people in the past was the most reasonable assurance that He
would continue to do so in the future

A Trio of Commands

Look at Israel's history! One thing is written and even plowed into it
that Israel should never forget—the impotence of idols! Whether Egyptian calves, Canaanite fertility godesses, or Babylonian images, they all
failed their devotees when the crisis came. Israel's God, however, has
always cared for His people. Although the verb translated "remember"
is fairly common in the Hebrew language, the "stand fast" has been
rendered several ways. The word is in the reflexive imperative form and
comes from a word whose root is not found in the Old Testament but
is most likely from an Arabic stem which means "to make firm," causing
one translator to render, "put yourself on a stable foundation." The
second imperative certainly strengthens the first. If the people would
consider the weakness of the pagan gods and the constant strength of
their own in history to deliver His people, they could certainly have
found the rationale for deepening their personal commitment to the One
who had sustained them through His endless resources.

The third imperative, traditionally rendered "bring it again to mind,"
is in the Hebrew the commonly used word most often translated "turn"
or "return" plus the noun usually rendered "heart." To bring it into
English as "cause to return to the heart" would perhaps best express the
phrase, but even "heart" does not fully convey the word's meaning since
this noun stands for the entire personality rather than only the emotional
part of one's being. The trio of commands demands that the people
whom the prophet called "transgressors" give serious consideration to
the spiritual issues facing them at this critical time in their nation's
history. Why did the prophet use such a strong word to describe these
people who were in danger of forgetting God's great deeds of the past?
Because failure to believe constituted rebellion of the worst kind. Such

an attitude flaunted the covenant relationship that existed between Israel and her God, causing her to lose footing. As Israel scoffed at her Rock in the days of Moses, she was in danger of doing it again. Such an attitude is sin of the sharpest kind—a transgression against both law and love.

No One Like Israel's God

Legitimate religious faith enables us to separate essential spirit from its causual forms. Experience, however, often makes it difficult to do this since we are tempted to mix the two, failing to arrange each according to its ultimate worth. Time should put issues in their perspective but sometimes it does the opposite. Unfortunately we sometimes have more true insight in our younger years than when the "evil days" come upon us. In verse 9, God through his prophet made two statements about Himself. First, He is the true Sovereign above human beings or anything we might invent to serve as god. The explanatory phrase which contends "there is none else" appears in emphatic form in the Hebrew text. Second, God asserts with finality that He, to use Delitzsch's expression, "unites in Himself all divine majesty by which reverence was evoked." As in the preceding phrase, the negative "there is none" is placed first, giving emphasis to it and answering the question "To whom will ye liken me?" raised in verse 5.

The revelation God made of Himself in the Egyptian Exodus was but the first of His mighty acts. As divinely caused events unfolded through the years, the faith and consciousness of Israel's spiritual leaders enlarged, and the significance slowly emerged in the minds of the serious thinkers. The prophets who came on the scene expounded the developing meaning of the covenant relationship. In fact, the Hebrew word translated "and" (v. 9) contains the idea of "significance" as the consequential importance of God's salvation deeds in history were expounded. The prophets regarded any event through which they were living as much like a coin. They at the time saw only one side but they knew it had an *aharith* on the back—its deeper implication or eschatological significance. These spokesmen for God were far more interested in spiritual principles, that a thing *would happen* than the exact year in which it would occur. The imperatives move into participles, and the prophet represented God as "declaring," literally "causing to be clear," the end from the beginning and "saying" that His purpose is fixed, and no contingency can make void that which He has determined shall occur.

God Uses Unlikely Instruments

The prophet could bring no more positive proof of God's hand in history than the fact that He could use a "vulture" like Cyrus to help bring about His redemptive work in the world. If such a man could be a part of God's plan for even a limited moment, so can every "villain" who has lived serve in some way to implement the divine purpose. In our own personal lives, we cannot always see God's hand at work when some devilish adversary seems to triumph over us. Great faith is required for us to see that the Lord may use an irritable, scheming, and sometimes destructive coworker to force us to examine our position, purify our motives, and refine our immaturities so we can at a later time be of maximum effectiveness in our work. Though some scholars feel "ravenous bird" was used to describe Cyrus because he moved rapidly in his irresistible attacks upon his enemies, the idea of *scavenger* is in the word and cannot be ignored in exegesis. The "man of my counsel" (v. 11) does not imply that Cyrus shared the ethical character or moral integrity of Israel's God but rather that he was the one whom the Lord chose as His instrument. Though Cyrus was unconsciously accomplishing God's plan, he had in mind his own ambitions. Perhaps he had "method in his madness" since liberating Israel and sending her home provided a buffer state between him and Egypt as well as projecting for himself an image of being tolerant to the gods of other nations which probably did him no harm in his political and military career.

Stubbornness of Israel

Knowing from her history that God works all things "together for good" to them that love him, Israel's unbelief could be called nothing but "stubborness of heart," and the prophet addressed the people this way. The Hebrew word rendered "stout"—applied to Israel's attitude—comes from a verb that means "strong." In some contexts, the idea is that of boldness or courage, but here it means defiance against God. One form of the verb means "to fly or soar," and this idea could be present with the prophet meaning they go into "fantasy flights" of their own importance, but more likely the idea of "tough minded" conveys the actual thrust of the word as used here. The people resisted God and opposed His plan because they were rebellious. One scholar, however, who took the "soaring" interpretation, suggested a double pun is present with the prophet's nuance meaning that the nation thinks it is God's Mighty One and was "clearly . . . soaring on its own pinions . . . ignoring the vulture whom God had decided to use." One outstanding rabbi, however, stayed with the traditional interpretation, calling Israel "perversely obstinate."

Such people could never take the initiative in either bringing or recognizing salvation. Much discussion has taken place among scholars as to the correct meaning of "far from righteousness" in verse 12 that describes the people. Most likely, the prophet referred to deliverance which is a synonym for "salvation," another idea of righteousness. In fact, the Hebrew words for "righteousness" and "salvation" are so closely related in concept that often they seem to be used interchangeably. The thought is that the people, because of their sin, are so far removed from righteousness that they have no power to effect their own deliverance. Such an interpretation certainly agrees with the New Testament teaching that man, in his natural state, is so deeply immersed in his depravity that he can do nothing toward bringing about his personal salvation. He must be saved by an act of grace!

A Triple Hope

Three beautiful and meaningful words, like a diamond flashing varying prismatic hues from its different facets, stand together in significant sequence as the prophet closed his oracle. Righteousness! Salvation! Glory! The emphasis is not on what persons have done but rather on God's gracious act. He calls it "my righteousness" for it proceeds from Him. This triple hope, rapturous and impossible as it seemed while Israel remained in her rebellious state, could become a sober certainty and a historical reality only because of God's redeeming grace.

First, of course, God's true character must be manifested. No one can receive the benefits of God's grace until that person recognizes the moral holiness that resides in the Creator and Redeemer. No cheap and easy transaction ever proceeds from God! Sin must be recognized for what it is, that which destroys everything good and decent. Also, an earnest desire to forsake it, which we call repentance, must precede any blessings that come because of God's unmerited love and favor which we call grace.

Deliverance follows! Though one may have felt God tarried, salvation was there all along if the people could only have seen. Long before Cyrus appeared on the scene, the people could have been delivered if they had only shown evidence of genuine repentance. God's words to Jeremiah when the prophet visited the potter's house show He always stands ready to "repent" if the people show evidence of moral integrity and an earnest desire to return to God's standards. God also has a free will! The prophet said for God, "At any moment I may threaten to uproot a nation or a kingdom, to pull it down and destroy. But if the nation which I have threatened turns back from its wicked ways, then I shall think better of the evil I had in mind to bring on it" (Jer. 18:7-8 NEB).

Repentance of Israel

A problem emerges at this point. Did the people actually repent? Not really! God delivered them for the sake of His redemptive work, not because they as a nation showed any evidence of change or "brought forth fruits meet for repentance" as John the Baptist later challenged people to do. The only unconditional promise God ever made to anyone was that He would send a Redeemer that would make it possible for the world to know of His grace and glory.

An old allegory from another culture, not too far distant from that day, would have horrified the prophet. According to this ancient religious tradition, people press upward from all sides of a mountain on the various roads of religion to meet God at the last and greet each other at the peak. Thus, according to the fable, all will eventually clasp hands in brotherhood and deliverance from their shortcomings. Not so, the prophet would have shouted. Man does not search for God. God has already taken the initiative. He has revealed himself many times—to Abraham; to Moses in Egypt and at Sinai; to the nation through many providential acts constituting what theologians call "salvation history!" We who are Christians maintain the climax in the revelatory process was at Bethlehem, Calvary, and the Resurrection. Israel had no need to search for God. He had already found her, chosen her, and had for a long time been carrying her.

God's Motive for Saving Israel

Back to the problem. God was about to deliver Israel for one reason—so that His redemptive program could "get back on track," looking forward to the day that the Word would become flesh and dwell among humanity. The truth of the prophet's message, brought over into the Christian context is beautifully expressed by the one who wrote:

Israel had been discovered by God and enlisted for a special mission.

For this purpose, and this alone, God was about to deliver her. She did not merit salvation as a nation, but God was ready to bestow it on her so she could serve as His agent in bringing deliverance from sin to the nations of the world.

What about the "glory" of which the prophet spoke (v. 13)? God placed His salvation in Zion so Zion could reveal His glory! The people, and perhaps the prophet, would have had difficulty, at that point, in understanding that the true Zion was not national Israel but the redeemed group who, in Christ, would receive the promises made to Abraham (Gal. 3:16). God's greatest glory is not physical Israel but those who received His Son as Lord and Savior. No obstacle that any person, in the prophet's day, might have placed in God's path could have prevented the fulfillment of God's incomparable plan of worldwide salvation. The Messiah would come! In God's time, of course, but He would come! Though the vision tarry, wait for it, for it will come! Regardless of the application to national Israel of that day, the message was most uniquely for individuals—as such invitations have always been and always shall be. God does not save nations but individuals. Even if an entire political unit seems to be going "down the drain," those people who in any generation repent and receive God's redemption can be saved. Today, if you will hear His voice, harden not your heart!

7
A Tale of Two Cities
(47:1 to 48:22)

In his classic novel about London and Paris, Charles Dickens began with a striking statement concerning opportunity and one's present day:

It was the best of times, it was the worst of times, it was the age of wisdom, it was the age of foolishness, it was the epoch of belief, it was the epoch of credulity, it was the season of Light, it was the season of Darkness, it was the spring of Hope, it was the winter of Despair, we had everything before us, we had nothing before us, we were all going directly to Heaven, we were all going directly the other way—in short the period was so far like the present period that some of its noisest authorities insisted on its being received, for good or for evil, in the superlative degree of comparison . . . It was the year of our Lord one thousand, seven hundred and seventy five.

What do you suppose the thinkers and writers in Babylon thought during those last few years before Cyrus the Great invaded the city. Perhaps some of them said of their nation what John Randolph of Virginia said in 1829 concerning his own—"The country is ruined past redemption"—or what Chancellor Kent of New York said in 1832 when he "threw in the towel" and complained, "We are going to destruction." Do you suppose any Babylonian editor commented on the year 539 BC as one American wrote of 1867, "a year of disenchantment, remarkable for the number and magnitude of illusions which have perished in it."

Pessimistic and paranoid pronouncements about one's present plight have not been confined to America. In 1848, Lord Shaftesbury said, "Nothing can save the British Empire from shipwreck." In 1849, Disraeli said, "In industry, commerce, and agriculture, there is no hope." In 1852, the dying Duke of Wellington said, "I thank God I shall be spared from seeing the consummation of ruin that is gathering about us." In 1801, Wilberforce said, "I dare not marry—the future is so unsettled."

In 1806 William Pitt said, "There is scarcely anything around us but ruin and despair."

Every generation has had those who felt their world was on the edge of a precipice. Often, they were wrong. With Babylon, however, things were different. They had come to the end of their rope. Midnight was but two minutes away! Cyrus was knocking at the door and about to knock it down.

In order to interpret this symphony, I find it necessary to "block off" certain sections and consider them as separate units. Various scholars approach the matter differently, making it difficult to be entirely satisfied with any division of the material. Chapters 47 and 48, however, seem to "hang together" as presenting a contrast between Babylon and Israel with God's final word being that of an assurance to Israel that, in spite of her sinfulness He was now ready to set her free and send her back home where she might once more make an earnest effort to be that which God wanted her to be—the instrument of the Lord's redemptive program for the world.

I. The Mistress Who Misbehaved (47:1-15)

No beauty in all the world can match that of a lovely lady! The Semitic world recognized this fact and always spoke of their cities as feminine. What stands more attractive to the materialistic mind than the skyline of a metropolis with its gigantic buildings? What thrills and challenges the heart which seeks to serve with compassion those who have special needs more than the congested streets where cross the crowded ways of life? Indeed, cities are a nation's delightful daughters!

That which is beautiful or has the capacity for beauty, however, when perverted, becomes the ugliest and most reprehensible! So with Babylon! She was at one time mistress of the world, capital of the greatest empire. Her glittering civilization, urbane culture, and favorable climatic conditions for agricultural fertility, combined with the financial resources produced by such a mixture made Babylon indeed the ideal of "position-seeking" people among the nations. Her mighty temples, exquisite palaces, colonnaded sacred streets, and the Gate of Ishtar that pierced through the inner wall have all been verified by modern archaeology. Her ugliness, however, was that she had no heart. Not a trace of the slums where the poor lived in hovels can be found among the ruins. Why? Because these homes of the underprivileged were built so shabbily they

disappeared completely and forever when the ravages of war destroyed
the city. A nation where a few grow rich at the expense of the milling
masses is ugly no matter how magnificent the high rises appear to the
stranger who views them for the first time.

Payday Had Come

Judgment time had arrived for the queenly city! The prophet proclaimed doom upon the bloated empire which had seemed to stand so
secure. No longer could she bribe enemies with her extreme wealth nor
buy mercenaries, providing what has been called the "sinews of war." In
an apostrophe, Babylon was addressed as the seat of the empire and her
humiliation was pictured as that of a delicately reared female suddenly
reduced to disgrace.

Nothing quite like this chapter appears in the prophetic symphony.
Thus far, each unit of Scripture has built upon the previous one and
contributed to the next as the various themes unfolded. The pieces fit
together like a mosaic to create a larger pattern. In this proclamation,
however, we have a long, unbroken scene in which the prophet, speaking
for God, thundered forth to a proud and confident Babylon that her fall
and utter humiliation were certain. Power is the most dangerous poison
to the soul of a nation because an exalted ego takes over in such a way
that the people cease to be aware of what is happening when they are
trampling over the little people in their own land and the larger world.

Previously Unconquered

Why was Babylon called a virgin? Most likely because she had never
been subjected to a foreign power. The Hebrew word is not *almah,* the
one used in the prophecy to Ahaz (Isa. 7:14) which is translated by most
scholars today as *maiden,* meaning a young girl of marriageable age, but
bethulah, the word that specifically means one who has never known a
man sexually. Babylon had never been ravished but she would be soon!
The three imperatives in verse 1, two of which come from the same verb,
command the proud, queenly nation to descend from the heights of
imperial power to the status of a country with no royal house, a ruler
with no throne. Even if Gesenius was correct in contending that the word
virgin daughter means not merely the city but the whole of Chaldea, there
is no great change of meaning. Instead, the consternation intensifies.

Countries are often personified by their capital city. As it goes, so goes the nation. When the chief city falls, the entire nation topples with it.

When the prophet spoke of the fact that Babylon would be no longer called "tender and delicate" (v. 1), he may have been alluding to the effeminancy and corruption of morals which prevailed in the city, making it sought eagerly by those who wished to engage in licentious indulgences. One Old Testament student said that descriptions of life in Babylon recorded by two separate historians in other languages were so vile that he refused to translate them into English and include them in his commentary. He said the conduct was so loathsome, disgusting, and abominable that nothing like it prevailed even in any other of the most corrupt nations of antiquity.

Exposed to Shame and Toil

Six feminine imperatives make verse 2 ring with urgency and shocking pathos. The prophet spoke against the background of the slave handmaiden, engaging in the most menial tasks. Simple peasants formed the proletarian substructure of Babylonian society, and the women toiled in the filth of the suburban areas which were intersected by little irrigation canals. Women puddled through those ditches tramping on the family wash. Millstones were commonly used for grinding the meal with the lower one convex on the upper side and the upper one concave on the lower side. Grinding, usually performed by the women, was often regarded as a slave's work and frequently inflicted as punishment. Veils and trains were worn by women who were not required to do the lower tasks. The head was the location of female modesty. She kept it covered, but when women went into captivity, the covering was removed as a sign of her abject condition. Scholars disagree on "uncover the leg" with some connecting it with the stripping of the train. The women were often required to lift up the skirt, thus revealing the leg, as they crossed the streams going to work although we should not rule out the fact that the prophet could be referring to Exile. The point of the six commands is that the nation was no longer a great mistress but an exposed and humiliated slave with some of the figures even suggesting that of a harlot.

Little, if any, comment needs to be made on the figure of speech in verse 3 where the prophet spoke of Babylon's nakedness being uncovered and her shame being seen. She had appeared outwardly as a powerful nation, but her true inward condition—emptiness—would be revealed.

Babylon had met one stronger than herself—not Cyrus, but Israel's God! He was now ready to take vengeance. The phrase "will spare no man" has been variously translated. Without attempting to list the various conclusions of scholars, we can safely say that the prophet meant no person, either through physical opposition or spiritual intercession, could have delivered Babylon. She was doomed! Her day of judgment had come, and no one could turn it back!

Either the redeemed Israelites or the prophet himself burst forth at this point in response to the Lord's declarations in the first three verses. This expression of admiration, grateful surprise, and recognition of God's power stands apart from the context but is a logical word at this point. Many scholars regard these words as a chorus that breaks in upon the subject, celebrating and praising the God of Israel for His mighty deliverance. Since the word *Redeemer* appears first, the emphasis is on that aspect of God's work. Whether the expression "Lord of hosts" (v. 4) is an allusion to the star worship of Babylon is difficult to ascertain. All hosts belong to God and are subject to His control. The "Holy One of Israel" holds forth the truth that Israel's deliverance is spiritual rather than merely political. As Redeemer, God has the power to do for the people that which they need. As Lord of hosts, He wills to redeem them and as their Holy One, he accomplishes this redemption in righteousness and moral purity.

A Call to Mourning

Though most scholars see verses 5 through 7 as a section in which God gives the reason why He must humble and punish Babylon, the first of these verses virtually repeats the command in verse 1. The prophet ordered Babylon to assume the role of a mourner for defeat, degradation, and death were coming. The anguish and grief that would be hers would be "poetic justice" for she had grieved Israel for years. The paradox was that Israel's calling was to bring others from the realm of darkness and hopelessness. God's strange ways of grace are revealed here. Since Babylon's heart was hardened from sin, she lacked the ability to understand how God would work with Israel. Therefore, God must drag Babylon down to the dust and overwhelm her with His judgment before she would be able to possess the insight necessary for redemption. To put it another way, Babylon's eyes must be blinded before God could use His servant Israel to lead her to the truth. One scholar put it beautifully when he said that "only when a man is walking in the darkness can the Light shine upon him." Babylon must come to the place where she was no longer called "mistress of the kingdoms" before she could be a part of God's kingdom.

Folly of Reformers

God intended to punish Israel because she deserved to be reprimanded and purified. He chose Babylon to do it, but that nation abused her commission. She executed God's sentence but did so with pride, ambition, and severity. Babylon, therefore, must suffer the rebuke and wrath of the One who chose her to do His punitive work. Though God had decreed His people must suffer for their sins, this did not justify Babylon's cruel and heartless spirit. A great lesson emerges for us all at this point. Reformers often become carried away with their zeal even when they are doing something that God has called them to do. Jehu, for instance, pleased God in that he "broke the back" of Baal worship in Israel and eliminated Ahab's family from the nation's throne. For that, God promised him four generations on the throne. However, he followed the same policies as those initiated by Jereboam I, setting up altars at Dan and Bethel which displeased God. Even such great reformers as Uzziah, Hezekiah, and Josiah seem to have become "puffed up" with a sense of their own importance in their latter years. Uzziah usurped the function of a priest, Hezekiah showed a flippant attitude when Isaiah accused him of indiscreet conduct with the emissarries from Merodach Baladan, and Josiah thought he could defeat the Egyptian army at Megiddo for which he paid with his life. Babylon was not conscious of a command from God to discipline Israel but could not have done it without his help. Remember what happened to Sennacherib! Babylon merely felt that what she was in her strength, she would always be! What a terrible thing for any of us to assume!

Babylon's False Security

Though the prophet, in verses 8 through 11 continued to hold before the people of Babylon the causes for their coming punishment, he particularized the type of calamities that would overtake the people, intermingling causes and effects into an artistic literary stanza. Several modern translations render "thou that are given to pleasures" (v. 8) as "voluptuous one," a good translation since the verb root means to be soft, lax, pliant, and from this comes the idea of to live luxuriously. Because of her imagined security, Babylon spoke of herself the way God did of Himself, frivolously claiming deity, and daring in her self-confidence to oppose all other gods. Feeling assured of her position, she asserted with defiance that she would never know the two greatest calamities that can befall a woman, loss of husband and loss of children. The fact that the prophet changed from the figure of a virgin being ravished to a wife and mother being made desolate poses no problem. Literary style is not an end in itself but a means of expressing truth.

Imagined Aids

What were these "multitudes of sorceries" and "abundance of . . . enchantments" which Babylon employed in an effort to secure favors from the gods? Since men of that day lived so close to the soil, the peasant way of life depended upon the annual crops. These forces of nature seem to die in the summer but are revived in the October rains. To the Babylonians, the gods had died and must be resurrected. The people felt that by engaging in certain ceremonies, which became increasingly immoral as the years passed, they could create life in nature even as the sex act can procreate in the human realm. This degenerate religion caused Babylon to believe she could never become a widow nor be childless because she herself could bring life through her religious cult and the ceremonies accompanying it. She had male consorts without number for these sexual orgies, trusting this wickedness and imagining that no one could or would take any action against her no matter how disgusting these mad and frenzied actions became from year to year. The phrase "none seeth me" (v. 10) does not mean Babylon thought no one knew about her conduct. That was a matter of open record. Rather, she felt no one could do anything about it or would even dare to oppose her.

To absolutize any ideology which the living God has created will lead one to the vicious spiral of a hardened heart and ultimately to express confidence in a blasphemous boast of pride. Babylon's inability to save herself or even recognize her need to be delivered stemmed to a large extent from her perverted philosophies which brought sophistication rather than true knowledge. Such people cannot see their real need and, therefore, have no capacity for repentance since they feel no need for it. Desolation comes suddenly and "that without remedy."

A Challenge and a Warning

With sarcastic irony, the prophet called upon the people to invoke the aid of those forces in whom they trusted (vv. 12-13) and then concluded with a description (v.v. 14-15) of how utterly impotent these pagan "diviners" were to effect any benefits for their constituents. One scholar suggests the "now" should be understood as more or less of a concession that the prophet realized they had become weary and perhaps have a "burnout" concerning these enchanters. Babylon must still have felt she could find deliverance through them, but the prophet knew they would never be successful. The "let now" of verse 13 repeats the essence of the previous statement. If the counsels stood successfully when the crisis came, they would prove themselves to have validity, but if they failed, the answer would be obvious. They were false teachers, without authority and without integrity.

What would be the fate of these in whom the nation had placed her faith? Immediate and evident destruction! The interesting combination of stubble and fire is not so much to show how worthless these false teachers are but to show how quickly they would be consumed. Also, though not definitely stated in the text, is the thought that the people who had trusted in these "phonies" would perish also. In fact, the last phrase in the chapter, "there shall be none to save thee," makes it clear that the nation, not merely the false teachers, was doomed. In the final verses, the prophet projected the idea of a besieged city, whose defendants were crazed with thirst and blood, surrendering to the attackers but finding no one to save or offer any kind of hope. Only Israel's God could prevent a body from atomizing and splitting up into its component parts, but Babylon showed no disposition to turn in repentance and call upon Him. Therefore, everyone would "stagger before him" and find their little worlds tumbling about their ears as they recognized they must face nemesis as a "disintegrated soul." Whether in the sixth century before Christ or in a day of technological warfare, the principle is the same. The one who sins will die!

Why will a mistress with everything act in such a way? Pride! A feeling of self-sufficiency and an attitude of "I need no one." A nineteenth-century poet put it this way:

> Out of the night that covers me
> Black as the Pit from pole to pole

I thank whatever gods there be
For my unconquerable soul.

In the fell clutch of circumstance
I have not winced nor cried aloud
Under the bludgeonings of chance
My head is bloody, but unbowed.

Beyond this vale of wrath and tears
Looms but the horror of the shade
And yet the menace of the years
Finds and shall find me unafraid.

It matters not how strait the gate
How charged with punishments the scroll
I am the master of my fate
I am the captain of my soul.
                              —William Ernest Henley

The factual reality, however is that we are not the "master of our fate" and never will be! God stands within the shadow always, keeping watch above His own, and our personal choice is the true determiner of our future. Choose God and live!

II. The Servant Who Sinned (48:1-11)

The worshiping community in Judah counted themselves as the true Israelites, and confessed their dependence upon their historic Lord, considering Jerusalem as their city. Why not? The Holy One of Israel had called it His city (45:13), and those who sought to serve Him should do no less. Logically, an oracle to the city of Babylon should be followed by words concerning the other city, Jerusalem, the place where God had put His name, which He had promised would in years to come be the center of world religion, and where He would reveal Himself in truth and righteousness.

Though Israel is not called "servant" in this particular segment of Scripture, previous references have made it clear that this designation is correct, and, in the latter part of this chapter, the terminology is repeated (48:20). In these verses, the prophet spoke directly to his own people and referred to them as those who "call themselves of the holy city" and depend upon the Lord (v. 2).

A Caustic Condemnation

With a direct approach that bordered on abruptness, the prophet began his message. He was speaking, he claimed, to people called by the name of Israel and the true representatives of the messianic strain, for they were the tribe of Judah. Yet they had failed to keep their moral integrity but rather were people who worshiped falsely and without ethical character. This chapter is more than a series of widely differing oracles, fragmented pericope, as some contend. Rather, the message is a unity and no reason can be found to regard it as anything except a sermon delivered at a particular time and place in history.

In the first two verses, the prophet addressed the people directly, accusing them of hypocrisy and calling them to hear God's word and heed it. Combining the three names, Jacob, Israel, and Judah, the prophet made a significant point. The source of the present Israel was Judah. The word "Israel" is used in several senses throughout the Old Testament, paving the way for the great "spiritual Israel" concept of Paul in the New Testament. Historically, Israel from Jacob preceded all other names, but Judah was chosen as the tribe from which the Messiah would come. The word gradually took on an even deeper spiritual meaning although the beautiful name-changing experience in the patriarch's life was kept alive by the constant references to Israel. The prophet referred constantly to the fact of the people's religious heritage through the use of names, stressing that their God's grace was the reason they existed in the first place, and thus they should be anxious to serve Him and realize the goal for which He had called and blessed them.

No excuse for Israel! How could she be blind to the way God had heralded every major event in her history and then confirmed His word by bringing it into reality? How many times God had told His people that He would act for their salvation! By now, they should have taken Him at His word if He but whispered a truth.

Reason for the Signs

Why did God give such signs to His people? The prophet said God knew how stubborn the people were, calling them rigid as iron and unyielding as bronze (v. 4). Therefore, He told them in advance so that when it happened they would have no excuse not to believe Him and could not possibly attribute their deliverance to the false gods whom many of them had no doubt come to worship both before and during the Exile.

For those of us who live in the full light of Jesus Christ, a significant truth arises and can be clearly seen because we are familiar with our Savior's attitude toward signs. He told a group, "It is a wicked, godless generation that asks for a sign" (Matt. 12:40, NEB), quite a contrast to the many spiritually immature people of Old Testament days who constantly sought for an external confirmation to assure them they were making right decisions.

With all due consideration for the various ideas of scholars, the "new things" of verse 6 refers to the coming Exodus from Babylon. Though the "have showed thee" is in the perfect tense which denotes completed action, we should probably understand it as a prophetic perfect, something the prophet knew was going to happen and was so certain of it that he spoke of it as having been completed.

Had Israel heard of these things before or not? One scholar presented the contention that God gave them enough to let them know they could not attribute their coming deliverance to the idols but not enough to give them sufficient power to abuse the knowledge. Another added the thought that they "had heard, but they had not heard." God had given them the message clearly but, because of their sinful state and rebellious attitude, they had refused to hear, being spiritually incapable of discerning the truth because of their sins which produced a void of understanding.

God Must Honor Himself

Since Israel had been such a sinful servant, why had God not destroyed her completely? With a graphic parallelism, the prophet set forth the reason in unmistakable terms. He has a name that must be honored! Praise is due to Him that He must receive! Therefore, God will prolong His anger, exercising His patience and refusing to execute judgment. Further, He will muzzle Himself so as not to destroy completely the people and thus forfeit the praise He deserves. When God's love encounters human sin, we see divine wrath. Holy zeal must of necessity burn up and destroy anything which threatens to pollute such love. Yet this tension between God's mercy and His wrath does not always become so acute as to demand immediate action. Since the days of Moses, God had been "holding himself in" because He did not want to cut Israel off though He at one time threatened to do so and start again with the family of Moses (Ex. 32:10). He had sworn, however, to be faithful and loyal to Israel, allowing her to be the means of bringing salvation to the world. He must be true to Himself and His word! Otherwise, the very people he sought to win to Himself, the nations of the world, could and would scoff at the idea of His moral integrity and their need to worship and trust Him.

Not even a chosen people can scoff and mock God forever! He must act, and He did in three historic stages. Two deportations (605 and 597 BC) should have been sufficient warning, but they refused to learn. In 586 BC, the final blow came when Nebuchadnezzar sacked Jerusalem, burned the Temple, and carried the remainder of the population to Babylon, leaving only a few in the land. This action, however, was not to consume but to purify the nation. Most translators render the prophet's words in verse 10, "I have refined you but not as silver," but some have insisted on other meanings for the preposition. Such suggestions as "with" and "for" give various shades of interpretation, but the general message is not all that difficult. God had brought about the Exile to transform Israel not to obliterate her, and the refining process was the only course He could pursue.

How much heat does a refiner apply? Enough to drain away the impurities and allow His own image to be reflected in the metal. Beautiful thought! God only wished to see Himself in Israel so that she could then be a witness to the nations of His moral integrity and holiness of character. This is all God ever wanted in Israel. Is that asking too much? When the people in Jerusalem saw the boldness of Peter and John and realized they were not formally trained theologians, they realized the two apostles had been with Jesus (Acts 4:13). When a warm, compassionate minister who had worked closely with people including many college students passed away, there were many tributes about him. One student testified that he saw Christ in the life of Brother Bryan. God wants His own people to reflect His character, and be the medium of a revelatory witness. He refuses to allow any other nation that privilege which He had offered to Israel. He must, therefore, discipline her in the furnace of affliction so she could be "meet for the Master's use." The sinful servant must not only be forgiven but must be completely transformed.

III. The Lord Who Loves (48:12-22)

The old, racking problem of pain remains with us. Dean Church said that a fly may have as much success trying to get through a pane of glass or a man trying to jump into space as one who attempts to solve the dark enigma of pain. Halford Luccock said more recently, "The real tragedy in the world is not pain; it is sterile pain. It is the pain that has no fruit, no redeeming outcome." In a sense, the words of both men fit Israel in the Babylonian captivity. She neither solved the problem nor learned much from it. Nevertheless, God loves and still will redeem. Since He made the world, He can remake it and anyone in it. Because He was there at the beginning, He will be there at the end—and at every stage in between.

Israel's Present Problem

Knowing that everyone is more concerned about present problems and distresses than even the most glorious days of past history, the prophet leaped from creation to the contemporary scene that he might give full attention to the vital question of the moment—Israel's present plight and how she would be delivered. Most evidence supports "who among you" rather than "who among them" (v. 14) which indicates the prophet commanded Israel to gather and issued his challenge to her rather than to all the nations. Some scholars find it so difficult to think of God loving Cyrus that they manipulate the translation to make the text say that God "loves Israel and will do his pleasure against Babylon." To love and to choose are very closely related in Hebrew thought, and verse 15 seems to reaffirm the contention of those who insist the prophet was speaking of Cyrus as the one whom God had raised up to execute "his pleasure on Babylon," and be "his arm" upon the Chaldeans.

Though some scholars have trouble with the fact that in verse 16 a change of persons takes place within the verse, this should pose no problem. The prophets were so conscious they were speaking for God that often they varied "back and forth" between what they said and what they said that God said. They felt themselves to be so closely identified that they saw no inconsistency in bringing one moment a commanding word from themselves and then suddenly shouting "the Lord says," claiming for both statements the same source of authority. In the Hebrew text, the negative precedes the "from the beginning" which puts the emphasis there rather than of the fact that He had not "spoken in secret"

(v. 16) Of course, both are true, but the thrust is that God never has even from the start of His revelatory work ever hidden His message from the people. The idea may be that God was refuting the heathen soothsaying with its esoteric qualities. In such activity, the emphasis was on hidden mysteries made known gradually only to the initiates. Contrawise, Old Testament prophets came before the nations as forthright speakers on behalf of Israel's God. Delivering a proclamation stood out as the principal thing, being very practical and aimed at instruction so the hearer might understand the true character of God, thus becoming in a position to worship Him properly.

God Demands, But Redeems

Nowhere is God's love demonstrated any more in the Old Testament than in the plain way He taught the people. In verse 17, the prophet combined the didactic quality in God's character with His redemptive work. The same God who points out in unmistakable terms how the people should behave is also the One who will forgive when they fall short—providing, of course, that they come to Him in genuine repentance. Anytime God promises to forgive people as individuals, the offer is on the condition those persons will see the error of their ways and make an honest effort to come back to God in loving obedience. He redeemed the nation as a whole by His grace, though there was a minimum of national repentance because He was planning to use them as a corporate body to produce the Messiah. Even then, however, they were required to show an element of sorrow or at least have suffered in Exile enough to make them tender and pliable so they could once more resume their role as the "priestly" nation.

What Might Have Been

With a wistful expression of desire, God, through His prophet, poured out His heart in agonizing pain as He recalled what might have been if the people had been willing to accept their assignment and live according to God's wishes. How differently things could have transpired! Rather than being a stunted nation in a captive land, openly exposed to heathen barbarities, Israel could have been the pride of nations. Heathen nations could have been "bending before the God of love" because Israel had conveyed the message through her holiness. Part of misery is in "remembering former better days" or contemplating how present suffering need

not have happened if only one had acted on the knowledge one possessed.
O memories that bless and burn!

On Your Mark! Get Set! Go!

Something good is about to happen to you! The prophet shouted the
prediction in the form of a command. "Get out!" We need, however, to
discern the emphasis of the urgent plea. The main thrust falls not on the
getting out in a hurry for later the prophet said, "Ye shall not go out in
haste, neither shall ye go by flight" (52:12). Rather he insisted that the
people make a "clean break" with Babylon and all the evil associated
with that land. This separation from the second "house of bondage" was
but the first step in the new order of things that would culminate in the
Messiah's coming. The Israelites, therefore, must make this deliverance
known with "a cry" that by means of their proclamation the truth might
be known to the nations.

Regardless of how one might divide the remainder of chapters 40
through 66, a unit ends here! Many scholars propose a "three-act drama"
with the first act concluding by the great proclamation that Israel was
going home! In the first Exodus, God met the people's need by making
water flow from a rock. Once more He would provide by intervening to
bring rich blessings. When a Jewish scholar expressed surprise that the
Book of Ezra did not record the miracles which occured on the return
to Judah, a Christian scholar wisely replied that the prophet was not
describing in verse 21 a literal journey but something infinitely greater,
the deliverance which Jesus Christ, our Savior and Lord, accomplishes
when He delivers us from the bondage of sin. An even greater truth
comes when we see the language as figurative, with the description of the
Babylonian Exodus symbolizing the salvation which we have in God's
fullest revelation, the true Messiah, of which Cyrus was but a weak
symbol.

A Final Necessary Warning

Why did the prophet not close this section with the glorious picture
of the Messiah and the life He brings? The prophet felt a further word
was needed to those who refused the Lord's message. God will act in
history with the cooperation of those who follow Him but in spite of
those who refuse. The latter, whom he called "wicked," will know no
peace. To reject the wholeness and fullness of life, the true *shalom,* means

to refuse to be effective. Verse 22 is no editorial comment, as some would contend, by a pious scribe of a later day. The phrase is so important that the prophet later quoted himself (57:21). He reiterated for effect that which he declared in verse 1, wishing to awe his hearers with the fact that God determined to reveal His glory and accomplish His purpose despite the fact that the people as a whole had broken the covenant and departed from Him.

Thus, we have a tale of two cities, but more—a distinction in philosophies and a contrast in God's activities. Babylon deserved the punishment that came to her, but in reality so did Israel. Even though Israel's iniquity was not as disgusting as that of Babylon, she sinned against greater light and was at least equally guilty, if not more.

Why the difference in God's attitude? He had chosen Israel for a purpose. His promise to Abraham was not merely to make a nation great but to use a nation to make a great people, those who would find redemption in Jesus Christ. Certain blessings come as by-products when we are faithful in serving God and working out His purpose in our lives, but God chose Abraham to be a servant not an honored person. God redeemed Israel for His name's sake and to put her back "on track," pointed in the direction of that day when in "the fulness of time" (Gal. 4:4) He would send forth the Messiah, born of a woman and born under the law. He would redeem both those under the Mosaic law and those who knew not the law of Moses but knew the law written within their own hearts, the moral law which accuses us all when we violate it. Wickedness in any nation, city, or person, is an awful thing, but God's grace is greater than all our sin!

8
You Can Go Home Again
(49:1 to 52:12)

The exuberant theme of Israel as the Lord's servant comes into fuller focus as the prophetic symphony progresses. A line runs from the beginning to the end of Israel's history which binds all of it together—God's word to the nation revealing His purpose for humankind. From the beginning, He wanted Israel to have only one valid reason for existence—the instrument through whom He would bring His redemptive program to reality in history by sending His Son to be the world's Savior.

Sin Delayed God's Plans

Because of their sins, the people had suffered Exile, but God never forgot they were uniquely His. He had chosen Israel as the one to implement His plan but found it necessary to chastise her and purge the impurities from her repeated sins. At last, however, she was ready to go back to her homeland where she could begin again her pilgrimage to accomplish her chosen work. The material in 49:1 to 52:12 forms a unit which marks a distinct advance in the development of the prophet's concepts. The controversial tone of repeated comparisons between the Lord and the idols disappeared as the prophet changed directions in thought. He had made his position sufficiently clear and felt secure on the subject. The matter of Cyrus's work had been set forth and was taken for granted. The prophet was ready to concentrate his attention on the central message—consolation for the present and a glorious state for the future.

Analysis of Material

The prophet's message flowed in several directions, but an essential unity pervades the various passages. The first section (49:1-13) describes God's choosing of Israel and the duty He had assigned to her. He,

112

therefore, promised to restore the people. The message closes with a hymn of gratitude to the Lord, based on the prospect of deliverance. Next (49:14 to 50:3), the prophet assured Israel that God had not forgotten her, suggesting that she look around and note the events that showed clearly His activity in redemption which included giving the people their land back. The Servant then spoke (50:4-11), telling of His obedience in spite of the sufferings He had been called upon to endure. The Lord, at that point, resumed His words of comfort (51:1 to 52:12) which had been interrupted by the Servant's soliloquy concerning His adversities.

Though the final section continues to the fourth and final servant poem (52:13 to 53:12), the prophet's thoughts were occupied with the near prospect of deliverance, and his high-strung emotion issued forth in shortened impassioned words of a lyrical nature which many scholars see as a collection of small, separate oracles (51:1-8,9-10,12-16,17-23; 52:1-6,7-12). Some are addressed to desolate Zion, but others contain words of cheer to the faithful though timid hearts who have given an entrance to the prophet's words. Running throughout this entire section is the prophet's certainty that God's people could go home and were about to do so, this time led by God and protected by Him as before but without the haste necessary when they fled from Egypt.

I. Commission (49:1-13)

Though the Christian community lives in the full light of God's revelation in Jesus Christ, we have not solved the dilemma of predestination, foreknowledge, and free will. The Servant insisted that God had called Him from the womb of His mother (v. 1). This was in harmony with men like Jeremiah (1:5) and Paul (Gal. 1:15) who claimed the same distinction. Does this mean they had no part in the decision? We will leave this problem, for the moment with the theologians and major on that in the message about which we can be certain—God calls and we have the glorious privilege of responding affirmatively to His summons.

When a "hard-shell" Baptist asked a minister who sought to press the claims of Christ if he didn't believe "what is to be will be," the preacher gave a good reply. He said, "Yes, I even believe what is to be has been." The man asked, "What do you mean?" He quoted, "That which hath been is that which shall be; and that which hath been done is that which shall be done: and there is no new thing under the sun" (Ecc. 1:9). The man said, "I don't know what you're talking about." The preacher smiled, "I don't either. Now let's talk about something we do know about. Have you received Jesus Christ as your Savior and Lord?" Some things will never be understood on a human level. Paul wisely said, "O the depth of the riches both of the wisdom and the knowledge of God! how unsearchable are his judgments, and his ways past tracing out! For who hath known the mind of the Lord?" (Rom. 11:33-34).

The Servant Reappears

Who is the servant? As said before, the ultimate fulfillment of the servant passages is found in Jesus Christ. The prophet began, however, with the thesis that Israel was God's servant—which indeed she was in a very real sense. This section forms a natural sequel to 42:1-6, but some fresh features are added. In the former passage, the servant was spoken of, but in this one, he spoke for himself. In the first three verses he made it clear that the Lord had raised him up for a purpose. The two difficulties suggested by some scholars should give no problem. He did of course mention that he had failed in the past and did speak of restoring Israel when he in fact was Israel. If, however, we accept the thesis that the prophet had moved to say that not Israel as a whole but "Israel within Israel"—the spiritual nucleus of the nation—was the servant, both problems disappear.

In the past, the righteous group had, through the years, labored to extend God's sovereignty but had been disappointed with the shortcomings of their fellow Israelites and the rebellion of the nations. Also, the prophet felt that the righteous group within Israel must be the catalyst to restore the entire nation. Actually, the people, as a whole, never repented of their sins while in Babylon. God restored the nation for the sake of His servant David (37:35), which means in order to accomplish the redemptive plan he had for the world in bringing the true Son of David, Jesus Christ, to the spiritual throne of David which He occupies today.

The Three Israels

As we read such passages as these, we must be aware of three concepts concerning Israel. First, national Israel was uppermost in the mind of most of the prophet's hearers. He, however, came to see that "Israel within Israel" was the true servant. A third Israel emerged later, however, made explicit in the New Testament but certainly implicit even in this passage. Spiritual Israel, the ultimate concept, would be those who accepted the higher revelation of God which reached its zenith in Jesus Christ. The prophet had this group in mind when he said that God revealed to him that it "is too light a thing that thou shouldest be my servant to raise up the tribes of Jacob, and to restore the preserved of Israel: I will also give thee for a light to the Gentiles, that thou mayest be my salvation unto the ends of the earth" (v. 6). Though our Jewish friends saw and unfortunately, for the most part, still see only a nationalistic application to this passage, we who are in Christ see a far greater truth, made real in the life of Jesus. The words "Kings shall see and arise; princes, and they shall worship" (v. 7b) refer not to a Jewish kingdom either without or with Christ but to the universal body of believers which would become a reality in history because "the Lord/has chosen his servant;/the holy God of Israel keeps his promises" (v. 7c). Unless one sees our Savior and His spiritual kingdom in this passage, the whole point is missed.

God Speaks to the Servant

Turning from words about how God had called and equipped His servant, the prophet pictured the emancipation of the Exiles and their return home. He spoke as though the deliverance had come, but the complete speech shows the event was still in the future. Beginning with verse 8, the prophet, speaking for God, addressed the servant directly. God had chosen the time for the working out of His plan and would act when He chose. The "I have answered thee" (v. 8) suggests the servant had prayed for restoration and perhaps means further that the spiritual nucleus had asked for God to use them to extend His rule in the world. An earlier writer had told how God promised the new king, "Ask of me, and I will give thee the nations for thine inheritance,/And the uttermost parts . . . for thy possession" (Ps. 2:8). Since most scholars see a messianic thrust in this psalm, we will not go wrong if we suggest that the prophet may have had this request in mind as he addressed the servant in his day.

Since the prophets always spoke in terms of their own historical context, this one promised Israel that God would preserve the nation, renew the covenant, and return the people to their land. He assured them of a safe journey home with necessities provided for their comfort. Every obstacle would be removed, and their fellow Israelites from all places would join them when they arrived. This was the people who would then fulfill His plan, the Israel in whom God would be glorified or, as the literal Hebrew says, "in which he would glorify himself" (v. 3). God had placed the responsibility upon them. They must accept their task and perform their duty as all good servants do when they understand what their master expects from them. God had called Israel, equipped her, and kept her ready for the time when she would assume her obligation and discharge her duty in a way that would be pleasing to Him.

A Lyrical Outburst

Following the frequent custom of the prophets, God's spokesman burst forth into song. The prospect that he saw opening before his people convinced him God's love for persons had triumphed. He addressed the heavens, earth, and mountains with the jubilation of a man who, though he still travelled in darkness as far as the outward situation was concerned, walked not by sight but by faith in the unseen. The prophetic perfect tense that the prophet used showed he believed so firmly that God would do what He had promised that he spoke as though God had already done it. Though the usual translation is "hath comforted" (v. 13) many scholars believe the Niphal form suggests a "reestablishing." This "once-for-all" act followed by the imperfect form "will have compassion," which speaks of continuous and repeated action, represents an ecstatic proclamation to the discouraged and sometimes unbelieving community. God had chosen His servant and outlined the servant's duties. He would see to it that the work was completed!

In every generation, God calls His servants to proclaim salvation to the nations. These messengers must decide whether they will be heralds of a local god of limited salvation to an exclusive group or view the world as their parish. They must be motivated to look beyond their regional horizons and see that God in Christ demands that His servants leave their little interests and localities to go to the larger world of people. Religion, to God's servants, must be more than a private hobby to develop their own spiritual lives. They must take upon their hearts, deliberately and decisively, the entire world's need for Christ. James Smart said, "No man with the New Testament in his hand can have a moment's hesitation about the answer." He quoted Augustine who said, "What I live by, I impart." Whether the world hears and heeds is not the question. God's servants must deliver the message faithfully. It is not necessary for God's servant to be popular. It is necessary that the people see Christ. To be a servant of God is a thrilling and noble enterprise. It demands and deserves every part of a person's being in uttermost self-commitment.

II. Consolation (49:14 to 50:3)

Having established the servant's commission, the prophet turned from ecstatic proclamation and rejoicing to a dialogue with the unbelieving community. Some scholars see four fragmented oracles in this section (49:14-21,22-23,24-26; 50:1-3) placed together because of kindred subject matter to form a literary unit. Others insist the material is a continuous message delivered by the prophet on a specific occasion to an audience. Whichever view one takes, a high view of Scripture and inspiration can be maintained. We shall never know exactly how the prophetic books were compiled nor is it required to accept their spiritual truth and authority. God spoke through the prophet, and His message was preserved for our edification. A thematic unity exists as the people raised a question, and the prophet, speaking for the Lord, answered.

The complaint was the same as on other occasions. Israel felt God had not dealt fairly with her, that He had forgotten them and cast them off completely. All four of these oracles, if we accept them as multiple messages, deal with this same subject, answering the people's charges against their covenant God.

God's Maternal Love

The Lord's first answer (vv. 14-21) was to compare His love with that of a mother for her child. This remarkable figure of speech occurs a number of times in the Old Testament. George A. F. Knight contended it balances the usual masculine image of the Almighty that people have held through the centuries. He said,

If only the early Church had fed the ordinary believers faithfully with the truths of revelation as they are given us in the OT, as well as with those that come to us from the NT, the felt need for a mother image in the heavens would never have developed, and the Virgin Mary would not have been exalted to the position she now holds in the imagination and respect of many. In fact, the Virgin Mary is really the representative of the feminine figure of Zion, the people of God, of the OT.

Whether or not one accepts this observation, the metaphor is striking. The Lord's remembrance of Zion, the place where He dwells, is more enduring than the strongest human affection. The most unlikely contingency we can imagine is that of a mother forgetting the child she has nursed. Though Israel seemed to be poor, abandoned, and helpless, God had not forgotten and would not forsake her. Two other figures follow quickly. He had engraved Jerusalem upon the palms of His hands. Some contend this picture was suggested from a Babylonian practice with which Israel was familiar. They tattooed the name of their god upon their hand to remind them to whom they belonged and who was the controlling power in their lives. The statement that Jerusalem's walls were continually before God may refer to the ruined walls which served as a silent appeal to the Lord's compassion. More likely, however, the prophet meant God had in mind a plan for the new walls which would be built. This was fulfilled of course in Nehemiah's day, though a previous attempt was made before that time.

The Repopulated City

Beautiful as the reconstructed city with its walls and buildings may have been, the city's real wealth would be in her sons and daughters who were God's children. The prophet saw a multitude of people inhabiting Jerusalem and saw those who had sought to oppose and mistreat Israel vanishing. To have many people possessing a land was considered a blessing for large populations were necessary to till the land and protect the people from being exploited by enemy armies. The prophet's picture of the repopulated city arrayed in beautiful garments and ornaments as a bride stood in sharp contrast to the daughter of Babylon who had been previously stripped naked of all that showed her to be a queen (47:1-3).

The same God that had laid Jerusalem waste would bring new life to His chosen city. Though He had been forced to put away His bride for a season because she was unclean, had consorted with other lovers, and had given her loyalty to others, He had long ago swore He would give His glory to no other person or people than His bride whom He had chosen. This bride, who had become a widow, would once more be filled with inhabitants so numerous that living space would be a problem. The mother's amazement was not meant to be absurd but rather to emphasize the miracle which would take place. God would make that which was humanly impossible become a reality. George Knight saw this as an act of grace, a combining of *agapē* and *eros,* in the love of God for Israel.

He compared it to the birth of our Savior produced in a human body but sired by grace through the Holy Spirit.

Israel Honored by Others

The first of the three short oracles (vv. 22-23) continues God's plan for restoration of His people. The Gentile nations would be the bearers and nourishers of the returning exiles. At a signal from God, these Gentile people would assist in the redemptive plan though they of course did not understand their part. To lift up the hand was a sign of beckoning or inviting. The standard or ensign was erected during war as something around which the people could rally. God would use both of these to call the Gentiles to take part in His efforts to spread true religion to the world.

Though the picture of the nations bringing their children in the bosom seems in a sense symbolic, a literal element is present. When in later years the Gentiles would become a part of God's kingdom in Christ, they would bring their little ones for instruction in the Christian faith. Kings and queens would later protect both the Jewish and Christian faith, especially the latter, becoming indeed "nursing parents" for the Lord's people. Though some modern minds find the exaggerated expression of humility, "lick the dust of your feet" (v. 23) as objectionable, to the Oriental it meant only complete subjection. We should remember that the nations were pouring out their devotion not to national Israel but to her God. Complete obedience on Israel's part would cause a self-emptying to take place that would leave no room for national status or pride. Of course, national Israel never came to that place. Only in Jesus Christ do we see the true faith breaking national barriers and even then it was difficult for many of the early Jewish Christians to see the universal nature of Christianity, apart from Jewish rituals and ordinances.

God Fights for His People

The next oracle (vv. 24-26) raises a rhetorical question and then draws a tremendous lesson from it. God had made great promises to His people. Could He fulfill them? To do so would involve taking the prey from a mighty conquerer and delivering the captive from the strong. This was seldom if ever done. The prophet insisted that no doubt existed as to whether or not Israel's God was strong enough to do it. Such an action from God would represent even less than full justice for the evil thoughts and plans of those who had conquered Israel. Because God was living and active, He must do something to vindicate His holiness even if it was shocking and unbelievable.

The fate of those tyrants who had oppressed Israel has been offensive to some modern expositors. They have accused the prophet of lusting for bloody vengeance and giving divine sanction to such cruelty. He was merely, however, using terms common among the prophets to describe civil war (Isa. 9:20; Zech. 11:9). God destroys ruthless tyrants by letting them destroy themselves. Unlimited egotism and power always brings conflict with its own people, bringing defeat. Evil is always its own executioner.

Israel Still Belonged to God

Next (50:1-3), the prophet dealt with a doubt the exiles must have had concerning the covenant relationship between God and Israel. Had Israel, in her sin, broken it beyond renewal? Two illustrations from common life assured her no such thing had happened. First, the Lord had not divorced Israel. According to Jewish law, when a man divorced a woman and she married another, she could not later, if divorced from her second mate, return to the first. Of course, only the man could obtain a divorce. Further, no divorce became legal unless the husband presented his wife with a certification of the legal transaction. God's plan was to allow Israel to leave Him and then suffer her just punishment for unfaithfulness, but He vowed to take her back later. The story of Hosea and Gomer illustrates this truth.

Likewise, God had not sold Israel into slavery as a father might sell his children to pay a debt. *Selling to creditors* was a figure of speech for giving one into the power of a conqueror (Deut. 32:30; Judg. 2:14). The people rather had gone into captivity because of their own sins. They had disobeyed God and thus became bondpeople to a foreign power by their own choice. In expiation for her sins, Israel was thus temporarily sold to the enemy and banished from her homeland. God intended from the beginning to redeem her when the appointed time came.

The prophet expressed the Lord's lament and complete surprise that His message of redemption received so little enthusiasm. No one seemed to care when the pre-Exilic prophets warned, and few paid any attention to the Exilic prophets as they called upon the people to be faithful. They did not seem to realize how much God was hurt when they pursued other lovers and ignored their Lord. He had come to her in love, but no one answered. We see the empty home, the loneliness of God's heart, and the pain that dwelt in the center of His universe. This is of course the foretaste of a later theme—the lonely sufferings of the Messiah, our Savior. These words suggest the pathos of the New Testament statement, "He came unto his own and his own received him not" (John 1:11).

God's spokesman declared forcefully, however, that the Lord could have at any time done anything He wished, and He still has that power. The reason for Israel's Exile was not because of God's limited ability to save. At any time He wished, He could have thrust forth His hand and reached for His people. He possessed power over all the forces of nature as well as the world's inhabitants. Had He wished to do so, He could have produced darkness in the heavens and reversed the order of creation as well as His gracious purpose of creative redemption. To redeem the world that way, however, was unthinkable. God's method was to use a Servant dedicated to the task assigned Him. Any other method would have been unworthy of His character.

III. Consecration (50:4-11)

The servant entered! Unintroduced, he came into the conversation with his word concerning God's act of grace. This is the third of four poems concerning the servant that appears in chapters 40—55. Each moved forward as the prophet presented the servant concept progressively. At first (42:1-9), the servant was set forth as the nation Israel although the characteristics presented were fulfilled ultimately in Jesus Christ. Next (49:1-6), the servant became Israel within Israel. In this passage (50:4-11), the Servant is definitely an individual. Some feel the emphasis is on the servant as the prophet himself, but others feel he spoke of someone else. In the final poem (52:13 to 53:12), the Servant is definitely an individual other than the prophet. No one but Jesus Christ could possibly be the fulfillment, even temporarily or partially, of the fourth poem. Let it be emphasized strongly that the ultimate fulfillment of all four servant poems is found in our Savior. We are speaking in this exposition of the prophet's presentation to the people of God's progressive revelation of His redemptive purpose.

The Servant's Work

Completely dedicated, the servant spoke not of himself but of his Lord who had, through his grace, bestowed the gift of an effective tongue. How important is the matter of communication? Thomas Carlyle seemed to deprecate it by saying, "All speech and rumour is short-lived, foolish, untrue. Silence is our fundamental talent." But he also said, "The tongue of man is a sacred organ . . . If the Word is not there, you have no man there either, but a phantasm instead." One mission of the servant was to teach, especially to bring strength to those who were weary, refreshing them with a message from the Lord that He cared for them in their distress and inadequacies. How parallel to the Savior's ministry! The Messiah and His work are implicit in this passage regardless of the historical context in which the words were spoken by the prophet. James D. Smart said, "The true Israel across the centuries is one who has been wakened each morning to the word of God." We might add that the "true servant" also fits this category.

The reason the Lord opened the servant's ear each morning was so he could follow the example of the "learned ones." The purpose of God's work was not to impart knowledge for the servant's mind but to prepare him for obedience. The Old Testament's strength lies in its realism. Daily vigilance must be a part of our life's experiences if we are to serve faithfully in God's kingdom.

The Servant's Obedience

Beginning with verse 6, the servant presented details to show he was not rebellious. The graphic language calls to our mind the Lord's sufferings in the days of his flesh. The statement "gave my back to the smiters" makes it clear the servant was in control of the situation. Jesus said, "I lay down my life . . . No one taketh it away from me, but I lay it down of myself. I have power to lay it down, and I have power to take it again" (John 10:17-18).

Most people, in all ages of the world's history, see only one answer to the problem of commanding obedience. They believe you must strike your servant in order to make him comply with your orders or instructions. This servant, however, had learned from his Lord not to run away nor to rebel or even to hit back. Instead, he allowed himself to be abused. He boldly delivered God's message though he incurred persecution and humiliation. The most degrading insult the people of that day could perpetrate on one whom they wish to shame was to pluck the hairs from his beard. This was the way to render him inferior or "put him down." Spitting in the face is for us an act of the must vulgar brutality. In Israel, however, it was the customary way of humiliating the prisoner, even before he was brought to trial. When a man refused to accept the responsibility of a Levirate marriage to his brother's widow, she was allowed—perhaps even commanded—to spit in his face (Deut. 25:9). These indignities suffered by the servant suggest a Jewish judicial process. We are so accustomed to a society that shows respect for a person until he is condemned that we find it difficult to realize such things happened in that day in a court of law.

Suffering Without Complaint

The servant faced these insults without making any attempt to retaliate. He bore the shame and disgrace without complaint. George Adam Smith suggested there are three classes of people who suffer physical ill-usage at the hands of their peers: the foe in war, the criminal, and the prophet. He contended that history shows us the prophet fares by far the worst. Though men often treat their enemies in war with a certain code of justice and fairness, the prophet has in all ages been the target for the most licentious spite, cruelty, torture, indecency, and filth past belief. The servant, however, refused to seek an escape from the verbal insults, taunts, and degrading gestures.

The reason for the servant's steadfastness was the personal resources because of his relationship with his Lord. Only one who possessed complete spiritual security could undergo such sufferings without a rebellious spirit. In our day, we can endure tribulation with patience if we know God is watching over us with an approving eye.

Because of his complete trust in the God of Israel, the servant would allow no temptation to deflect him from his divinely appointed course. Obedience to God's will loomed paramount in his determination. His hard-set face could not be turned to one side or the other. The strong-willed servant resembled the spirit of the later Servant who, though He knew death faced Him there, steadfastly set His face to go to Jerusalem (Luke 9:51).

A Challenge to the Opposition

Adopting the courtroom format, the servant challenged anyone who opposed him to take legal action. He knew the Lord would stand beside him as his Advocate. Paul conveyed this same attitude as he shouted, "Who shall lay anything to the charge of God's elect? . . . who is he that condemneth?" (Rom. 8:33-34). The servant knew that the accusers would take so long to make their case that they would wear out like a garment. The "moth" metaphor suggests the deteriorating process that would come to those who sought to harm God's representative.

The prophet gave a fitting conclusion and summary as he addressed first those who feared the Lord and then those who opposed him. Though a few scholars interpret "he that walketh in darkness, and hath no light" (v. 10) as referring to the servant, most see it as designating those who fear the Lord and obey the voice of His servant but have no light because God's revelation has not fully appeared. The exhortation to trust the Lord and maintain implicit faith thus applied to the followers of the servant rather than the servant himself. Fearing the Lord and obeying the voice of His servant go hand in hand because God's will had "materialized" in the voice of the one He had chosen to execute His will. In obeying the servant, one would find himself leaning upon God, trusting not merely in the servant but in the Lord God Himself.

Warning to the World

A final message was reserved for those who opposed the servant and his Lord, mainly the pagan world. The prophet associated the corrupt deeds of his and the Lord's enemies with the kindling of a fire which may have some reference to a ritual connected with pagan worship. If so, he seized this figure and turned it swiftly into a metaphor which pictured God's judgment. The figure of sin as its own executioner occurs often in the Old Testament. A similar, though not identical passage, "Just as straw is set on fire by a spark, so powerful men will be destroyed by their own evil deeds, and no one will be able to stop the destruction" (Isa. 1:31, GNB) conveys the same thought. Evil people have no light except their feeble and glimmering torches, and the only future for them is fiery torment. Though the moral law of the universe operates to produce such a condition, God stands behind this law and thus the prophet was incontestably correct when he said for the Lord, "This shall ye have of my hand; ye shall lie down in sorrow (50:11).

IV. Consolation—Continued (51:1 to 52:12)

In his classic *You Can't Go Home Again,* Thomas Wolfe said,

You can't go home to your family, back home to your childhood, back home to romantic love, back home to a young man's dreams of glory and fame, back home to exile . . . back home to cynicism, back home to aestheticism . . . back home to ivory towers, back home to places in the country . . . back home to the father you have lost and have been looking for, back home to someone who can help you, ease the burden for you, back home to the old forms and systems of things which once seemed everlasting but which are changing all the time . . . back home to the escapes of Time and Memory.

In a sense, of course, he was right. Life moves on, and the tomb of time buries all things. With God, however, a "land of beginning again" is always available. Joel promised the people of his day that the Lord could restore the "years that the locust hath eaten" (2:25). Israel was going home, and in this section of Scripture the prophet made it clear God was going to start afresh with them and work out His purpose that had seemed defeated forever.

A Command to Faith (51:1-8)

Interpreters vary in analyzing this larger section with some considering it a single discourse while others view it as a number of separate fragments. Though we shall treat it as one continuous word from the prophet, we shall note the separate trains of thought but, nevertheless, see the unity of the message. In the first smaller section (51:1-8), the prophet gave a glowing and animated appeal for those exiles who believed in the Lord to put away the fears and misgivings which hindered their full acceptance of the salvation promised to them. George Adam Smith called this section "Doubts in the Way of the Return" and pointed out that since God had answered their doubts of His ability to save them, they fell back upon doubts about themselves.

In order to bring reassurance, the prophet, speaking for God, called upon the people in his first exhortation (vv. 1-3) to look to their roots and see from where they had come. From one couple, Abraham and Sarah, they had grown to be a great nation. Though they were now fewer in number than they were before the Exile, they had the same God. He both could and would transform the waste places of Jerusalem to gardens of joy and make the uninhabited places like the original Garden of Eden, a paradise on earth. The nation was reduced to a mere handful, under the tyranny of power that seemed to be overwhelming. Rescue seemed impossible!

The Lord, however, challenged them that before they took a defeatist attitude they should go back to the beginning of His dealings with them. True, they are only a handful, but they are more than they were when God started His redemptive program through them. Alan Redpath made a very timely application to our day when he said,

Consider some of the words used: *waste places, wilderness, desert:* does that describe you? Is that your life . . . He asks you, therefore, today, if you are discouraged as a Christian and on the point of giving up, to look back to the pit from which He dug you, and to reckon upon His unfailing love.

George Adam Smith likewise spoke with relevance,

When we are weary and hopeless it is best to sit down and remember. Is the future dark: let us look back and see the gathering and impetus of the past! We can follow the luminous track, the unmistakable increase and progress, but the most inspiring sight of all is what God makes of the individual heart; how a man's heart is always his beginning, the fountain of the future . . . Lift up your hearts, ye few and feeble; your father was but one when I called him, and I made him many!

Having assured the people their land would be restored, the prophet urged them (vv. 4-6) to see the moral and ethical implications of the restoration, declaring that though the physical elements were dissolved, God's righteousness would never be destroyed. Why was God about to restore Israel? Not to build her own national kingdom, exclusive and isolated from the other nations! Rather, to serve as a place from which God's will for people reflected through the *Torah* would be disseminated to the nations of the world. God's whole cosmic movement depended upon Israel's giving ear to her God.

Though Israel's obedience to God seemed but an obscure act in an obscure moment in the history of an obscure people, yet through His providence that faithfulness to Him could mean the salvation of the world. Without it, the great and sovereign God was limited and could not act even as He could not have begun His plan without the obedience of Abraham or someone in His place. He could set before the people the authoritative expression of His will, which is the true meaning of *Torah,* but He needed His servant Israel to interpret this truth to the nations so they could and would become a part of His Kingdom on earth. Such words as *justice, righteousness,* and *salvation* demonstrate clearly that He is not interested in national boundaries or ethnic distinctions in His worldwide plan but only justice brought by moral and spiritual integrity. These traits characterize His rule upon earth. The Kingdom is within! Heaven and earth shall pass away but God's *Torah* remains!

The third earnest appeal (vv. 7-8) reaffirms God's power over the finite things of earth. Since Israel had God's law in heart and knew of His saving activity, how foolish for her to fear "short-lived man!" The Hebrew word is not *adham* but *enosh,* the term that emphasizes humanity's weakness and dependence. As the enemies of God would perish, so also would those who reviled His people. The prophet used two figures of speech to characterize the transitoriness of Israel's foes. They were like a garment eaten by moths and like wool devoured by worms. The context suggests that the deterioration process had already begun. The wicked people bore the seeds of their own destruction within themselves. Sin is always like that, but God's salvation shall never pass away for it stands rooted in His righteous character which is absolute and unchangeable.

The section which follows (51:9-11) shows the prophet adopting a new role. Where he had been the herald of God's salvation and spokesman for God to the people, he became the intercessor for the people with God. When he called out to the "arm of the Lord," he was actually speaking to the Lord Himself who controlled all the power residing in His person. He appealed to history. Though many scholars see a double reference to the Lord's previous work, one in creation and the other in redemption from Egypt, the case for the former allusion is doubtful at best. Assuming for a moment that the Genesis story of creation borrows some figures of speech from Babylonian origin stories, an assumption with which of course many disagree, the evidence is not convincing that the prophet in this context was referring to the subterranean sea monster slain to conquer the primevial depths and produce an orderly world from chaos. Every point of these verses applies easily and with clarity to the redemption from Egypt and is best interpreted this way. Rahab was a common term for Egypt (Pss. 87:4; 89:10; Isa. 30:7).

The day of redemption that had dawned for the present Israelites would parallel the previous one and was guaranteed by it. Israel's God possessed resources sufficient for the occasion regardless of Babylon's strength. He could use the "arm of Cyrus" to be His arm and cause His will to be done.

The lyrical outburst (v. 11) that concludes this section may be regarded as God's response to the prophet's prayer or the prophet's excitement as he saw the coming redemption. The fact that this same rejoicing appears almost exactly word for word in 35:10 is taken by many as an argument in favor of the same author for both sections of the book. Others, however, suggest this could well have been part of a larger refrain used often by the people during periods of separation from their "holy place" during and even before the Exile. Whatever the source and whoever the spokesperson, optimism must have been evident and enthusiasm great as the community realized their Exile was nearing its end, and they were about to return home.

In the third section (51:12-16), the prophet spoke God's message to Israel once more, continuing the words that ended at verse 8. Though the theme was the same, he treated it differently. The word *comforteth* with which he began is the same Hebrew word as in 40:1. The English translation is too weak to carry the prophet's meaning. We need a word that speaks of deliverance from despair into confidence and hope. Fear of human enemies undermined their confidence, and the prophet once more dwelt upon the mortality of those before whom the people trembled. The switch from second-person plural *you* to a collective singular *thou* suggests God comforts the people one at a time and then expects them to respond in His service as a body. George Knight contended the doctrine of the "church" is firmly rooted in the prophet's words, pointing out that *ecclesia*, the Greek word for "church," even as "Israel," the Lord's bride in the Old Testament, is both singular and feminine.

The nation's basic problem was that she failed to remember her God's creative work but constantly feared those who were seeking to destroy her. John Skinner pointed out that the "hast forgotten" (v. 13) should not be understood as falling away from God as much as failing to realize His omnipotence as Creator of all things. One result of forgetting is to think we can do all things in our own strength. Another, however, is to think we stand helpless before our opposition. The latter was Israel's greater problem at that moment.

A rhetorical "where is the fury of the oppressor?" (v. 13) was the prophet's way of pointing out the folly of fear. The word picture is that of an enemy preparing the bow and adjusting the arrow to shoot at the people. The question implies the enemy's wrath would vanish, never to appear again. God not only comforts but protects His people in their time of critical need.

Changing from a warning to a promise, the prophet pictured Israel as a captive to whom the doors of prison had suddenly been opened, giving her full freedom. The Hebrew word translated "loosed" is considered by some to mean "marching," but one must change the vowel pointing to gain this interpretation. No justification can be found for this on scholarly grounds. Only if one thinks he understands the passage better than the Massoretic scholars should the word be changed! The word rendered "pit" is not the one for Sheol though most scholars feel the prophet meant for it to be understood as a part of that nether world. No theological point is involved, and the main thought is that the exiles would not perish from isolation, exposure, or lack of food. The image conveyed reminds us of Jeremiah in the dungeon (38:9-10).

In order to pledge the integrity of His promise, the Lord, through the prophet, called attention to His power (v. 15) and the revelation of Himself (v. 16). This combination of controlling the elements and honoring the covenant served as an appending of His signature to the guarantee He had made. The God who could create a storm could also act with the gentleness of a softly spoken word, reminding one of the discovery Elijah made when in a state of depression (1 Kings 19:11-12). In *History and Theology in Second Isaiah,* James Smart said,

This close association of creation and covenant suggests that the word God spoke in the creation in order to bring order out of chaos is the same word he speaks not only to Israel but through Israel to the world that he may bring a new order out of the fearful chaos of the present. The creative power lies in God's word, so that a people with this word hidden in its heart has within it the power to transform the world.

How ridiculous that such a people signally blessed and divinely endowed with dynamic resources should be frightened by the puny power of ungodly men!

Following his custom of shattering contrasts, the prophet returned to the thought of 40:1-2. Jerusalem's period of shame and degradation had expired. Moving swiftly from Jerusalem as God planned for her to be, he revealed the actual condition of the city. He called upon her to rouse herself and realize she had received the fullness of God's wrath. In the section (51:17-23) he gave a twofold picture. First, (vv. 17-20), the city was depicted as a drunken woman with no one to lead her home. Both moral collapse and material distress had come to her. Everything in the city spoke of decay and ruin! Second, beginning with verse 21, a promise was sent forth. Though the city was in a drunken stupor, God remained her lover and faithful husband. He acted as a doctor would to an unconscious and dying patient. He took "the cup of staggering" (v. 22) from her hand and promised she would no longer be required or even allowed to drink from it. Rather, He would pass it to those who had acted brutally against her. God's wrath was about to end and His mercy to begin. He would not only deliver Israel from her heavy distresses but would place upon her enemies the calamities with which she had been afflicted. Great is God's mercy and great is His avenging wrath!

Though a chapter break occurs, the thought continues as in the next section God made even greater promises. Jerusalem was told to put aside her soiled raiment and emblems of slavery for bridal attire. This time, however, an even greater promise was made. Nothing degrading or offensive would enter the city. Since the cup of indignation and humiliation had passed from her hands, Jerusalem was ordered to shake off her stupor. Though Israel had up to this time been a worthless, fruitless bride, better days were ahead. No longer would she be enslaved but, because of the Lord's saving activity, she would be free to accomplish His redemptive will.

God would control the coming liberation completely. No price had been paid by anyone when Israel went into captivity. Therefore, the Lord owed no nation for her release. When they went to Egypt, the action was voluntary, but no cost was involved. The Assyrian invasion was to exploit the people. The Babylonian attack and deportation was the same. The Lord's question "What do I here?" (v. 5) is literally "What to me here?" and should most likely be understood as the Lord asking what He must do in the situation at hand. The logical answer was that He must deliver His people. A picture of the tragic condition that existed follows as the Lord pointed out that the captors were dealing harshly with Israel and God's name was being dishonored. As long as the people were in bondage this disrespect of the Lord would continue for Babylonian leaders had nothing but contempt for Israel's God even as they did for the gods of other nations. The section closes with a firm resolve by the

Lord that He would see to it that His name was vindicated which implies, of course, that He would act decisively to free His people.

The lyrical outburst which opens the final section (52:7-12) reveals the full dimension of God's salvation. The vivid pictorial imagery carries us back to chapter 40, but one great difference is evident. Since the God of Israel is the only true God, His sovereignty could not be limited. The liberation of Israel would be the prelude to the liberation of the whole captive human race. The first part of chapter 52 is limited, saying only that no heathen would be allowed to come into the city. The larger truth is that God's redemptive program will not be complete until all nations come to the knowledge of the Lord. In fact, this truth is implicit in some passages that seem to be entirely nationalistic. Those who had spiritual insight perhaps understood that when the prophet said the glory of the Lord would be revealed and "all flesh shall see it together" (40:5) he spoke of a turning to Israel's God on the part of many Gentiles.

From the beginning, God had in mind the whole world in His Kingdom, not merely a Jewish population. He told Abraham that in him would "all the families of the earth be blessed" (Gen. 12:3). In the return from Babylon, the Lord would make bare his holy arm "in the eyes of all the nations" and all the ends of the earth would see it (v. 10). The prophetic perfects show the speaker's certainty that these events would take place. He saw them in his mind's eye as already having been accomplished. God's kingdom not only would not perish, it would be enlarged to include people from all nations. What a marvelous foreshadowing of the Kingdom of our Lord Jesus Christ in whom there is no east, west, north, or south but one great fellowship of love throughout the whole wide earth!

A series of imperatives gives the final word to Israel. Get out! Get out! As you go, purify yourselves and refrain from anything that would compromise the holiness of the Lord! Had the city already fallen to Cyrus or was that event merely about to occur? We cannot be sure, but the prophet's cry was for those who had the freedom of choice, when the time came, to go home and start once again being a part of God's redemptive plan for the world. We cannot emphasize too strongly that this was Israel's role in history. God had not chosen her to magnify her as a political entity but to use her in bringing the world a revelation of Himself and salvation from sin. Only as we understand Israel in this manner do we understand her!

A comforting message ends the section. The people could take time to observe the laws concerning holiness and rituals concerning cleanliness because the Babylonian Exodus would be with quietness and dignity. The same God who preceded the Israelites in their march from Sinai to Canaan would be both before them and after them in this new endeavor. The symbolic presence of God in the Ark of the Covenant and pillar of cloud, as in the first Exodus, would give way to His spiritual presence without tangible externals. Nevertheless, God would be with them! He was endeavoring to teach them what Jesus said years later to the woman of Samaria, "God is a Spirit: and they that worship him must worship in spirit and truth" (John 4:24).

Though the historical facts of Israel's Babylonian Exodus thrill us, the more relevant truth of these chapters is the application to our own day and our present needs. Two great lessons stand above the exegesis to give strength for living today. First, nothing is more beautiful than the life of someone set free from the captivity of sin and the by-products of personal transgressions. Frustration, defeat, loneliness, and hell itself result from rebellion against God's will. Liberation brings happiness and joy, giving new meaning to life. Second, the last verse in this section promises Israel and assures us that God will be both vanguard and rearguard in all events as we march forward in accomplishing what we understand to be God's purposes for our lives.

Enslavement takes many forms, but God's redeeming grace is sufficient for any contingency. Temporary panaceas give limited solutions, but complete and permanent freedom comes only when a transforming experience produces a lasting liberation. God has spoken with authority in the resurrection of Jesus Christ and released a power into the world that has changed the lives of millions. This truth serves as the basic thesis of God's kingdom on earth. Paul expressed it succinctly, "He rescued from the power of darkness and brought us safe into the kingdom of his dear Son by whom we are set free, that is, our sins are forgiven" (Col. 1:13, GNB).

Three words used often in the Bible to describe life are *battle, voyage,* and *march.* William James said, "If this life be not a real fight, in which something is eternally gained for the universe by success, it is no better than a game of private theatricals from which one may withdraw at will. But it *feels* like a real fight." Henry Van Dyke represents those who spoke of life as the passing of a ship across seas which today may be smooth as glass and tomorrow tossed with a hurricane—till the harbor lights appear on the other side and the desired heaven is won. He eloquently said, "In thee we trust, what'er befall/Thy sea is great, our boats are small."

Perhaps, however, the picture containing the widest appeal is life as a march. When we put our ear to the ground and listen historically, we hear the tramp, tramp, tramp of humanity's hosts. John Bunyan spoke of the road beaten bare by the passing of pilgrim feet. Matthew Arnold pictured humanity marching in a long interminable column across the face of the ages. Many straggled and fell out, others grew faint and dispirited, but the march went on and the columns pressed forward.

Those times when God seems to be absent from our life's plans may be when He is most present. Early in his life, Oliver Cromwell, disgusted with the way he felt the king and court of England were ruining the nation and leading it to decadence and disaster, decided to leave the country and never set foot in it again. Inspired by those who had previously adventured on the *Mayflower,* he boarded a ship bound for the New World. At the last moment, messengers dashed up with orders from the king that he should not be allowed to sail. He felt all his life's plans had been ruined, but it was this seeming reverse that made it possible for him to become later the man who changed the course of England. When we stand before the dark mystery of the veiled future wondering what awaits us, we can cry, "Who goes there?" confident that the answer will be, "God goes there! Love goes there! Your Father goes there!" Both at the front and at the rear, God stands guard. Is this not sufficient?

You can go home! Home is freedom, and this is exactly what God wants for everyone of us. F. W. Robertson told of an insect imprisoned in wood. One day emancipation came when an ax stroke freed it. Light came in and then warmth, and the gauze wings expanded, the eyes look bright, and the living creature set forth. Its prison was not its home but rather the free air of heaven was its true dwelling place. Robertson said, "Christ taught that same truth of the human soul . . . It is never in its right place in the dark prison house of sin. Its home is freedom and the breath of God's life." This is what the gospel is all about! O what liberty a loosened spirit brings! When Christ makes us free, we are free indeed! In a sermon entitled "If I Had Only One Sermon to Preach," Paul S. Rees quoted James Stewart who said, "Why should we linger amid the shadows of the prison house when Christ's pierced hand has set wide the door?"

9
He Suffered, Bled, and Died Alone
(52:13 to 53:12)

Though most Christians speak of Isaiah 53 as the most outstanding passage in the Old Testament, telling of the Suffering One who bore our sins, this classic poem consists of five stanzas and actually begins with verse 13 of the previous chapter. This fourth servant passage climaxes the progressively revealed truth and adds a new dimension that sets it apart significantly as the picture of coming redemption which surpasses all the rest. Previously the servant was presented as the ideal prophet or teacher who was conscious of a worldwide mission in God's service. The servant's complete dedication to his goal gave unfaltering assurance that he would meet with ultimate success. The prophet gave no hint, however, in the first three poems that the servant's activity would be interrupted by death.

Necessity for Poem

Those who suggest these verses interrupt the context and could be eliminated without disturbing the flow of the prophet's message misunderstand the nature of the servant passages. They intentionally inject their truth into the ongoing symphony to open the door to the hearer's inquiry as to how God's great purpose in history would be implemented. A distinctive feature of all classical literature is that the soliloquy or oration is a necessary intrusion to set the stage for what follows and to tie together that which precedes. While chapters 40—55 might "make sense," and in some way even be a unit without the four servant passages, it would be voided of its overall truth and lack the very thing for which it was designed in the first place. This fourth poem is the heart of the prophet's message, and, without it, the very lifeblood would disappear.

Five Ascending Stanzas

The fifteen verses are divided into five stanzas of three verses each, but each one increases in length. This literary structure gives the solemn impression that the spiritual truth gathers more of human life into itself as it sweeps forward with fuller, irresistable volume. George Adam Smith suggested that the opening phrase of each stanza summarizes the meaning of the entire section and could well form a title for it. In a sense, this is true, but in some of the stanzas one must read further into the content to secure the ultimate truth although it may be implied in the opening phrase. The first stanza pictures the ultimate success of the Servant, and the next three describe the method by which He accomplished His goal. The final one returns to the original affirmation. The Servant will prosper, but the reason is given at the end—because He had sought to accomplish God's will for Him and His work. The three "middle stanzas" describe the Servant's alienation and substitutionary sufferings. The picture of Him as the One on whom God placed our iniquity when He was led as a lamb to the slaughter is fulfilled ultimately and only in Jesus Christ. Our Savior and Lord bore our sins in His body upon the tree that we, having died unto sins, might live unto righteousness (see 1 Pet. 2:24).

I. The Servant's Startling Success (52:13-15)

Since the words which followed would deal with the Servant's humiliation, the prophet began by proclaiming the ultimate triumph of this One whom God had chosen to implement His redemptive work. Also, the immediately previous picture of this Servant (50:4-6) contained unexplained and unvindicated sufferings. Knowing that the secular world is always success oriented, the prophet felt he should foretell the outcome before he described in detail the agony the Servant must undergo in order to deliver His people. These verses contrast His past and present plight with His future dignity and glory. The transformation of His fortunes, both marvelous and unexpected, would change the nations from amazement and horror to admiration and homage.

For the first time in the servant poems, we can say almost dogmatically that the Servant had become to the prophet a definite personality. Even as national Israel could not attain the role of Redeemer, though God chose her to be a "kingdom of priests" (Ex. 19:6), neither could Israel within Israel perform that function. This left an individual as the only one capable of wearing the title "Messiah" and implementing God's promise that through Abraham all families of the earth would be blessed. The prophet regarded the Servant as more than a passive agent, being rather an active and efficient force with the full initiative of a person.

He drew no line between the Servant's task on earth and the divine plan for all of creation. He could with full integrity conceive of the Spirit's clothing Himself with a man but at the same time putting on divine strength like clothing. Thus in harmony with this type of thinking we find the Servant described in both divine and human terms with no demarcation or contrast between the two. We who interpret this passage from the vantage point of Christ's resurrection see why His incarnation is the guarantee of and even the necessity for a divine personality. Unless we know God as a Person like us, we do not know Him at all. To lose ourselves in a law, tendency, moral impulse, or even a spiritual force is to lose ourselves in vain speculation. The Messiah must be a Person and so the prophet presented Him.

The Servant Would Be Victorious

The verb rendered "deal wisely" has been variously rendered by translators. Most today, however, see a derived meaning of "shall prosper," making a trilogy with an ascending climax—prosper, exalted, and lifted up very high. The prophet saw the Servant's career crowned with success. We should be careful, however, to avoid seeing this elevation as the effect of His own wisdom. A. B. Davidson said that the verse "is a simple prediction of the exaltation awaiting the Servant, in contrast with his past sorrows and abasement." God caused the Servant to be victorious! He would rise because He would not remain in His present state of humiliation. He would be exalted in that He would tower high above all else. The Christian interpreter, on reading these words, thinks immediately of Paul's beautiful poem in his letter to one of the young churches. He wrote of Christ Jesus who took the form of a Servant and became obedient unto death, but was highly exalted by the Father who gave Him a name above every name, declaring that every knee should bow to Him (see Phil. 2:8-9). The parallel is too evident to be coincidental. The Servant is Jesus Christ! No other!

God Uses Pain

Having made clear that the Servant would be exalted, the prophet introduced a contrast, addressing Him but with an objective tone. The two verbs rendered "astonished" (v. 14) and "sprinkle" (v. 15) set forth the distinction succintly. The masses of people were made to feel desolate as they viewed His sufferings, His countenance being more disfigured than anyone they had ever seen. Though God sometimes uses pain as a means of blessing His people and teaching them lessons, secular-minded people see pain only as a stumbling block and seek to remove it from their sight. They interpret suffering as a sign of weakness and inability to cope, sometimes even regarding it as proof that the "gods" are displeased with the person who is forced to bear it. When the world saw the Servant they staggered at the things that had happened to Him. Rabbi Slotki said, "His sufferings were so intense that their mark upon Him made Him lose the look of a human being." The quantitative contrast between "many" and "thee" often present in messianic passages dignifies the Servant as an individual, standing in contrast to those on whose behalf He acts but who have persistently misunderstood the redemptive nature of His sufferings.

"Marvel," not "Sprinkle"

Though scholars connot agree entirely as to the best rendering of the second verb, one thing is certain. The root idea of "sprinkle" simply does not fit the context. John Skinner suggested the word should be understood as having the causative thrust of a verb found in Arabic meaning "to spring" or "to leap" even as the English word *sprinkle* is perhaps the causative of "spring." Thus, the idea is "to cause to spring in surprise" or "cause them to rise up suddenly in reverential admiration." The Septuagint renders with a similar thought, "Many nations shall marvel." The people would be amazed at the Servant's sufferings, but they would also be astonished at His sudden and miraculous transformation. The "shut their mouths at him" (v. 15) confirms this interpretation, further substantiated by Job's touching description of the respect paid to him in earlier days, "The princes refrained from talking, And laid their hands on their mouths" (Job 29:9).

True Success

What is success? Many, sometimes even those in religious work, misunderstand success. A pastor in a large city, while caught up in the numbers game and enjoying external expansion of his church program but with little spiritual depth, wrote a book on how to be a great success. Ten years later his superficiality caught up with him. His marriage broke up, his questionable business dealings nearly "landed" him in jail, and he left the ministry. His "success" was based on a wrong concept of God's kingdom. Some of his fellow pastors met adversity as they sought to build their church programs on more stable though less spectacular methods and are still enjoying the fruit of their labors. Our Savior knew that true success was identifying with those who had needs. He was touched with the feeling of our own infirmities and was thus able to meet our needs. He did not seek to dodge the cross but faced it and used it as a lever by which to lift us to God's presence and power. This brings the kind of success that never perishes.

> Subtlest thought shall fail and learning falter
> Churches change, fanes perish, systems go,
> But our human needs they will not alter,
> Christ no after-age shall e'er outgrow.
>
> Yea, Amen! O changeless One, Thou only
> Art Life's guide and spiritual goal,
> Thou the light across the dark vale lonely,
> Thou the eternal haven of the soul.

This first section introduces the theme. God in His Servant revealed that, though many do not see it in their own experience, suffering is fruitful, sacrifice is practical, and pain in God's service leads to glory.

II. The Servant's Superlative Socialness (53:1-3)

The secular world associates leadership with charisma but almost always fails to recognize spiritual quality as the most dynamic of all traits for motivating people to worthwhile action. For this reason, those scholars who translate the opening phrase as "Who would have believed it!" have probably caught the exact spirit of the prophet's words. Whatever else we might say of Jesus Christ, He was no mere product of His day. We cannot account for His spirit and character by the world into which He was born. Nor can we entirely trace his teachings to any of the religions which at that time existed anywhere in the ancient world—including Judaism. He spoke with His own authority and not merely the borrowed decisions of the scribal schools. None of the nations knew the secret of the Servant's extraordinary powers of endurance and survival. He was unique, supreme, unequaled!

God's Strange Choice

Throughout the centuries God has often seen fit to do His work through those who seemed less likely to be His instruments. The twofold picture of the Servant shows His lack of charm or appearance. The "tender plant" was a sprout or shoot which sprang up when the ground was hard and dry. George Knight compared it to the "sucker" which grows from the roots of the rosebush, with thorns on its whole length. A good gardner cuts it out and throws it away. The "root out of a dry ground" (v. 2) parallels the first statement and is perhaps more accurately defined as that which comes up from the root, shoot, or sprout. The double figure presents the Servant as a spindly, unhealthy looking plant, struggling for its life in dry, hard-baked earth, in danger of withering and dying at any moment.

Of course, we should be careful not to develop the idea that the least attractive we are as God's servants in today's world, the more assured we can be that we are serving Him faithfully. Ellis Fuller once said in chapel at The Southern Baptist Theological Seminary that some people, because they read that Jesus said the world would hate you if you serve Him, rush right out to "make people mad at them" to prove they are in His perfect will. Such an attitude is foolish, but on the other hand the history of Christianity is indeed that of minority movements. Alexander Pope said forcefully, "He is a slave who will not be/In the right with two or three." The thrust of the statement that the Servant had "no form nor comeliness" and "no recognized beauty that we should desire him" articulates the fact that often we fail to recognize spiritual qualities in a person when we first see him. Some have trained themselves to have that insight. However, most require a time before they can appreciate the finer traits of character early in one's acquaintance with a person. Lusty vigorous growth is, according to James Smart, usually associated with pagan movements while steady, stable development is a characteristic of God's redemptive program for our maturing lives.

Specific Details

Verse 3 continues the community's repudiation of the Servant but moves from a general statement of humiliation to a more detailed description. The prophet gave more reasons for the Servant's rejection than mere surroundings or circumstances. He was so lowly and unattractive that people shrank from Him, never suspecting who or what manner of Being they saw when they looked upon Him. The picture is that of one whose rejection goes beyond the humiliation and pain Israel suffered in Exile. The Servant was wholly abject, having encountered evil in its most repulsive form. Not pain from natural causes, but rather because He had been disfigured by human malignity had caused Him to be shunned. The verse contains a series of verbs with the subject not being expressed except by implication.

The word translated "despised" conveys a stronger thought than "no beauty that we should desire him" in verse 2. The prophet's former statement is negative, but this one is strongly positive. The word is a participle with the force of an adjective. The same word is used with reference to Esau as he despised his birthright (Gen. 25:34) and Michal when she despised David (2 Sam. 6:16). *Rejected* means literally *ceasing* or *lacking*. The idea is passive—not that He avoided them, but they turned from Him. The same word was used by Job when he said that his "familiar friends have forgotten me" (19:14). The term for *men* probably means the "better class of men" rather than the common masses. *Sorrows* and *grief* are literally *pain* and *sickness* with the latter symbolizing sin. The thought is not so much that He was a diseased person as that He associated with those who needed His help because of their limitations. Though the grammatical construction will allow He "hid his face from us" or we "hid our faces from him," the latter seems to be demanded by the context. People found Him revolting to look at because He insisted on identifying with those who were enslaved by sickness and sin. They thus turned away from Him as though He had a loathsome disease. The verse ends as it begins with the prophet adding the tragic phrase "we esteemed him not."

The Grief of Greatness

Why was the Messiah a "man of sorrows"? His grief was the penalty for His greatness. His purity, enthusiasm, and love—these caused Him to suffer. His purity enabled Him to discern hidden sin with a holy sensitiveness though it hid in the moods and modes of virtue. His enthusiasm made Him unable to conceive of any person giving a lesser place to God's kingdom than He attributed to it. His love made Him susceptible to sorrow. Once a name is graven on our heart, we are open to the pangs and stabs of bitterness when death or disgrace comes near to that one we love. Jesus the Messiah was a human being in every sense of the word living in a society of real people to whom He related with divine love.

The unbelief which the prophet described is the same found all about us today. We may not hide from the victorious Christ, but we do turn away from the Jesus who gave Himself in redemptive selflessness. We want the triumph but not the toil that precedes it. We love the Lord of Glory but not the Suffering Servant. To put His teachings into practice would make us isolated fanatics. We do not want to lead the lonely path, but we must do it if we are to understand the holiness of His character, the mystery of His personality, the authority of His claim, and the message of His cross.

How withdrawn from normal society should one be today if he or she wishes to follow in the steps of Jesus? Each person must settle that in light of his or her own life and needs. We must be with people if we are to help them toward the Master, but we must be different from them if we are to impress them with their need of the Savior's forgiveness. The next stanza opens the door to a further understanding as it makes even sharper the contrast between the Servant's personal agony and the reason for His suffering.

III. The Servant's Substitutionary Sacrifice (53:4-6)

The most common moral judgment which people pass upon pain is that it comes as a punishment for wrongdoing. We suffer because God is displeased with our actions. Job's friends insisted God had struck him because of his sins. This was the first opinion of the people concerning the Servant—He was stricken of God and afflicted. The prophet had promised earlier, however, that he was about to reveal a new thing (48:6 b,16). Verse 4 begins a reinterpretation of the Servant's sufferings. This poem at first presents the Servant's death through the eyes of the unrepentant sinner. This stanza, however, gives it through the eyes of the repentant, forgiven sinner. To the traditional mind of that day, and even today in the secular world, God rewards and punishes to discourage vice and encourage virtue. A logic greater than human speculation, however, comes to the front in this evaluation of the Servant's sufferings. The righteous person dies the death of a sinner, and the actual sinner becomes righteous by beholding it through the eyes of faith and appropriating it personally. This rationale differs diametrically from that of those who are blind and deaf to God's great mercy and His way of reconciling people and bringing them to a new understanding of His divine purpose in the world.

Sin Makes God Suffer

Beginning with a particle best translated "surely," a grandeur is introduced as the prophet moved at once to the idea of substitution. Of all the theories of atonement which scholars have presented through the centuries to explain the death of Christ, that of substitution still leads the field of realistic theology. The position of the words in the sentence emphasize "our griefs" and "our sorrows" by which the sinful nature is characterized and symbolized through the use of nouns. A later prophetic word parallels this thought, saying that "in all their affliction he was afflicted . . . in his love and in his pity he redeemed them" (63:9). A combination of divine love and sorrow shines through these passages. As long as love's goal is not perfectly realized, sorrow enters and causes the idealist to suffer because of unfilled longing. God suffers when His creation falls short. Every time we sin, we increase the burden God must carry. In both Hebrew and Greek, the word translated in the Bible as *sin* means "to miss the mark." When we "miss the mark," the arrow turns aside and wounds God. Substitutionary suffering is not a concept unrelated to life but is at the very heart of our daily experiences. When we forgive a person who sins against us, we "bear that sin" in our own spirit.

Since sin is, according to Edward J. Young, something nonmaterial, how can one be said to bear it, he asked. Then he answered, "Sin involves not merely an inward corruption of the heart but also guilt before God." He maintained that the prophet, in saying that the Servant bore our sins, is in reality "declaring that he bore the guilt of our sin." Since, according to Young, even guilt is intangible, he contended that the Servant bore the punishment that was due us because of those sins. In other words, He was our substitute. Thus "wounded for our transgressions" and "bruised for our iniquities" mean He "bore the penalty that was rightfully ours." Accepting Young's interpretation, we may say with assurance that only one Person fits that description—Jesus Christ, our Savior and Lord.

Effect on the People

What were the steps in the people's understanding the true nature of the Servant's sufferings? First, they were *bewildered* by it. Next, they thought it was *contemptible,* thus passing an intellectual judgment. Since they felt they must find a moral reason for it, they decided it was *penal,* due the Servant for His own sins. Then they recognized the *vicarious nature* of it, having been enlightened by revelation through the prophet. Finally, they realized it was *redemptive.* The last two steps are stated as factual based on the preceding ones. Usually a prophet introduces strong pronouncements with "Thus saith the Lord," but this supreme truth which crowns the Servant's office is introduced by the lips of persons who have repented, not as a prophetic oracle but as a confession, the conviction of human conscience after the Servant had been lifted up before them.

The two words used for wrongdoing in verse 4 are strong and vigorous. *Transgressions* is the plural form of a Hebrew word that means rebellion or a sharp defiance of God's will. The word rendered "iniquities" has to do with moral corruption, having the picture of something warped or twisted. This word also contains the idea of the guilt associated with the action. The word rendered "chastisement" means literally discipline, and the thought is that of "pressed down like a burden upon the servant." Not retributive punishment but remedy or correction is suggested by the term. If peace is to exist between a person and God, a discipline must be placed upon the one who is estranged from divine favor. The healing produced by the stripes brings complete freedom from all things that caused the Servant to die. The verb is impersonal, being best rendered "by his stripes there is healing to us." Substitution permeates every part of the verse. The truth can be understood through no other figure of speech.

Why the Servant Suffered

A new thought emerges in verse 6 as the prophet told why the Servant was required to suffer—all of us had gone astray, like sheep, and were lost. One scholar of a previous generation said, "We walked through life solitary, forsaken, miserable, separated from God and the good Shepherd and deprived of His pastoral care." The pluperfect best renders the thought, "We had turned astray." The verb in the latter half of verse 6 has the force of hitting violently. Our guilt does not come back to meet us and smite us as we deserve and might expect. Rather, it strikes the Servant, not merely in the "soul" but in the whole person, the true meaning of the term. The Shepherd gives His life for His sheep. An old truism contrasts Old Testament religion and its sacrificial system with Christianity, "In the former, the sheep dies for the shepherd but in the latter, the Shepherd dies for the sheep."

An incident from my childhood makes this passage especially meaningful. One day as a ten-year-old boy, I was memorizing Scripture for an advancement project in church work. My father was following the text in the Bible as I quoted Isaiah 53:6. I made a simple mistake, saying, "the Lord laid on *us* the iniquity of us all." I still remember how my father corrected me. "Son," he said, "You missed it—not much, but you changed the whole meaning. You said God laid on *us* the iniquity of us all. If He had done that we would have all been helplessly and hopelessly doomed and damned forever." God laid on *Jesus* the iniquity of us all. Fifty years have passed, but I still remember my father's profound observation. It was for *me* the Savior died! He bore my sin and burden to Calvary and made them His very own!

IV. The Servant's Severe Suffering (53:7-9)

Where the main thrust of the previous stanza was on the vicarious nature of the Servant's sufferings, this one emphasizes the intensity of the pain. Added to this is the fact that the Servant refused to complain or object when He was mistreated. Twice in the opening verse the prophet used the phrase "he opened not his mouth." In this description of the meek and patient sufferer, we see prefigured the deeper aspects of the incarnation. God made Himself known to us in Christ who "suffered, bled, and died alone" and also without retaliating at any point toward those who brought agony and shame upon Him.

Agony Without Complaint

Silence under suffering is a strange and seldom-seen phenomenon in the Old Testament. Here, it represents a new development in the proper reaction to opposition and reproach. People of those days could not stay dumb under pain. They immediately broke out vocally in one of two ways, either in confessing guilt or challenging God in argument. David, Hezekiah, Job, Jeremiah—all of these great, godly men reacted loudly under pain. Why the difference between them and the Servant? The Servant saw behind the veil and realized a purpose was there—God's redemptive program in history. Thus, in the words of a New Testament writer, "for the joy that was set before him" He "endured the cross, despising the shame" (Heb. 12:2*b*, KJV).

The "He was oppressed, yet when he was afflicted" (v. 7) contains in the Hebrew text a verb, "was oppressed," followed by a conjunction and second person pronoun, "yet he," and concluding with a participle, "was afflicted." Scholars have rendered this in many ways. Both the verb form and participle have a passive thrust. The traditional translations, however, express well the basic thought. Even though the Servant was severely afflicted, He refused to fight back in any way, being humble enough to remain voiceless in the midst of violence. If we are inclined to wish He had spoken and called attention to His sufferings so we could remember them better, we should realize that the gifts of true love are never ostentatious. We usually conceal from those we love what it costs us to make them happy. A biographer of Lord Macaulay, telling of his dedication in working for the welfare of his brother and sister upon their father's business failure, concludes, "such was his high and simple nature, that it may well be doubted whether it ever crossed his mind that to live wholly for others was a sacrifice at all."

No One Realized or Cared

However we translate the "By oppression and judgment he was taken away," the basic thought is indisputable. The Servant suffered unjustly. Some feel the oppression was His "restraint" in prison while others suggest it was the fact that He was taken from prison unjustly, without a trial, and then put to death. The Servant died before the eyes of all, with no one but a small handful caring, or even knowing that a just person was dying for the unjust. Could anything else have been as heart-rending to the victim! No one considered or even stopped to think about the ethical or moral values of the case. He allowed Himself to be "cut off from the land of the living" for the sake of His people. No one took His life. He gave it gladly and without any sign of protest. A volunteer for the army during a fierce battle returned with only one arm.

Someone said sympathetically, "Oh, you lost your arm?" He replied, "No, I gave it." Jesus said, "I lay down my life ... No one taketh it away from me, but I lay it down of myself" (John 10:18).

The Servant's extreme suffering extended even to His death. However, His exaltation and glorification in a sense began with His burial. Some scholars disagree with the translation "with a rich man in his death," pointing out that though the primary meaning of the Hebrew word is "rich," the prophet undoubtedly meant for the two phrases to form a parallelism. We cannot say that everyone who takes this position wishes to minimize the prophecy's fulfillment in Christ's being buried in Joseph of Arimathea's tomb for even such a strong conservative as Delitzsch said that to take the two antithetically "they meant his grave to be with the wicked, but he was with the rich in his death" is entirely unwarranted. True, a secondary meaning of the word rendered "rich" is "arrogant" and one hesitates to disagree with such a man of reputable scholarship and integrity as Delitzsch, but translators as far back as the Septuagint saw this word as meaning "rich." Since it so beautifully portrays the historical facts about Jesus and since the natural meaning is "rich," we should stay with it unless further evidence is uncovered. The plural form of "death" in the Hebrew text emphasizes the intensity of the event adding to the thrust of this stanza.

No part of the Christian message moves one to belief and commitment more than the fact of Christ's suffering. An old truism says that it is impossible for love not to be returned. Whether we accept this or not, most agree unless we are entirely lacking in moral sensitivity such love will be returned. Jesus was more than a mere passive victim of God's wrath. The freedom and spontaneity of His sacrificing love constrains even demands a complete response.

V. The Servant's Supreme Satisfaction (53:10-12)

Though the opening words of verse 10 in the American Standard Version text come across as a grim and repulsive sound, the Hebrew phrase conveys no necessary meaning of pleasure or enjoyment. Rather, the prophet meant that what happened to the Servant was because God willed it. His purpose was in the tragedy. The sentence holds in perfect balance the problem of reconciling divine predestination and human free will. The American Standard Version phrase "Yet it pleased Jehovah to bruise him" does not mean the Lord found fiendish delight in seeing the

Servant suffer. Though His death was not in the hands of wicked persons but was God directed, a divinely planned program was taking place. Of course, this does not absolve the wicked people from their sinful deeds. They were in a sense not in control of their actions but, in another sense they were for they *chose* to crucify him. Great is the mystery of God's redemptive work. God used human wrath to bring about the means for reconciling sinful humanity and Himself.

Of course, the deed was dastardly and inexcusable! When we read of how cruel people crucified the Savior we feel as Clovis, King of the Franks, felt when he first heard the story. Drawing his sword, he shouted, "If I and my Frankish soldiers had been there, they would not have done that to Him." We must remember no caprice reigned in the deed—God did it deliberately because He wanted the world not only to see how terrible sin is but also for the world to be redeemed from sin's consequences. The Hebrew text is difficult in this verse, but one fact stands out inconvertibly. God's purpose cannot be checkmated by death, especially when God foreordains that death. We cannot understand or harmonize God's willingness to present His Son as a guilt offering for sin though He loved Him dearly and did not wish to see Him suffer. The Servant's freedom to be the sacrifice is set along side the fact of God's willingness to let Him be that sacrifice. This verse presents the will of God and the Servant's will coalescing, as in Gethsemane, not by compulsion but by the unconditional surrender of obedience.

Resurrection Clearly Taught

No tricky exegesis can eliminate the fact that a resurrection is taught in the latter part of verse 10. The Hebrew reads literally, "He shall see seed, he shall make long his days." The only way the Servant who was offered for sin could see the results of His work would be by becoming alive again. He found His reward for His work in the lives of those whom He redeemed. His seed are the true spiritual Israel, those who by His death and resurrection have been and are still being converted to God. Thus the cross and the empty tomb cannot be separated in Christian theology. They combine to produce an animating power that motivates to create a community of believers—New Testament Christians.

Edward J. Young said in the *New International Commentary* that "where the doctrine of Christ's satisfaction is proclaimed in its biblical fulness, there the true Church progresses." He added, "It is of importance also to note that the Servant himself will see the seed. If he were to die and remain dead, this would be impossible . . . death will not hold the servant, but rather, after his death he will again come to life and as a living one will see his seed." "Shall prolong his days" meant more than merely the resurrection. Included is the thought that He shall live eternally and evidently refers to the promise God gave to David and his seed (Ps. 21:5; 2 Sam. 7:13,16; Pss. 89:4;132:12). "In his hand" by which the Lord's purpose will prosper most likely refers to the Servant's hand rather than the Father's and may be understood as referring to the entire ministry of Jesus, though culminating of course in His atonement and resurrection. The Servant's work was not done in isolated activity but in communion with God the Father and His future seed the Father would give to Him. What supreme satisfaction came to Him because of His obedience!

Joy at the Result

As God exhibited satisfaction in His handiwork at the creation, so the Servant shall rejoice when He sees the results of His ignominious death and triumphant resurrection. The expressions "he shall see . . . and shall be satisfied (v. 11) and "he shall see his seed" (v. 10) are similar in sound in the Hebrew, and both stand in striking contrast to the Servant's lament in 49:4 that "I have labored in vain, I have spent my strength for nought and vanity" and His assertion that justice due to Him was with the Lord and His recompense with His God. Scholars differ as to whether the "knowledge of himself" which reads literally "his knowledge" is subjective or objective in nature. If the former, the emphasis is on the Servant's blessing the poor and weak with righteousness, bringing justice to the oppressed and equity to all. The latter, however, would emphasize the practical knowledge of the Servant by others that approximates faith. J. A. Alexander argued for the latter saying,

The only satisfactory construction is the passive one which makes the phrase mean *by the knowledge of him* upon the part of others; and this is determined by the whole connection to mean practical experimental knowledge, involving faith and a self-appropriation of the Messiah's righteousness, the effect of which is then expressed in the following words.

"He shall bear their iniquities" tilts the case toward a forensic justification format rather than merely a sympathetic identification with the weak and a desire to aid them in their quest for fair treatment from oppressors. George Adam Smith said,

It is a needful and a lovely thing to assist the feeble aspirations of men, to put yourself on the side of whatever in them is upward and living,—to be the shelter, as the Servant was, of the broken reed and the flickering wick; but it is more indispensable, and infinitely heavier, to seek to lift the deadness of men, to take their guilt upon your heart, to attempt to rouse them to it, to attempt to deliver them from it . . . man's supreme and controlling relation is his relation to God, and to this their *righteousness* the Servant restored guilty men by his death.

Victory Already Won

In the closing words of his book *God in the Slums,* Hugh Redwood said, "Christ is not struggling for victory. The victory was won 1900 years ago. That is what the ordinary man needs to be assured of—the daily victories of the Living God." The prophet closed the fifth stanza of this servant poem with a great affirmation of triumph. The phrase "divide the spoil" (v. 12) is a figurative and proverbial expression for victory or success. A wise man wrote, "Better it is to be of a lowly spirit with the poor,/Than to divide the spoil with the proud" (Prov. 16:19). The "therefore" with which verse 12 begins calls to mind the same word which begins Philippians 2:9 where Paul stated that the result of Christ's condescension is that God exalted Him and gave Him a name above every name. The Servant would be as successful in His mission as other conquerers have been in theirs, but His would be spiritual service rather than military conquest.

A Final Fact

A closing recapitulation tells why the Servant would be so gloriously exalted. He voluntarily exposed to be brutally killed on our behalf." George Adam Smith said, "Innocent as he is, he gives his life as satisfaction to the divine law for the guilt of his people. His death no mere martyrdom or miscarriage of human justice: in God's intent and purpose, but also by its own voluntary offering, it was an expiatory sacrifice . . . There is no exegete but agrees to this." The concluding conjunction *and* suggests a gradation. Christ both bore the sins of many and became an intercessor which work He is doing today. The priestly work of the Servant is thus emphasized. He pleads before God the merit and virtue of His atoning work. This is the only ground of acceptance before God of the sinners for whom He died. The substitutionary expiation of God's Servant is the only basis for the validity of His intercession. Worthy is the Lamb!

We Must Never Forget!

What should be our attitude toward the Savior who is foreshadowed in the five stanzas of this servant poem? We must never forget what He has done for us and continues to do! The secular world makes a strong bid for our time and attention. Spiritual discipline is difficult to maintain and impossible unless we remember constantly and meditate often on His sacrificial and substitutionary death. To hold in mind the sufferings of Christ will keep us from unbecoming conduct and unworthy attitudes.

In South Carolina after the Civil War, a retired general allowed his name to be put in nomination before the state legislature for United States senator. While serving under him, a man who had had a disagreement with him determined to oppose him and speak at length against him. When the man walked toward the speaker's stand, he saw a disfigurement on the general's face and remembered the day he had shown unusual bravery in hand-to-hand combat, saving many lives including possibly his own. He stopped and shouted spontaneously, "I can't go against him. I forgot about the scars." Rather, he gave a strong supporting speech for his former "army boss." We need a similar attitude toward the suffering Savior.

> See from his head, his hands, his feet
> Sorrow and love flow mingled down.
> Did e'er such love and sorrow meet
> Or thorns compose so rich a crown?
>
> Were the whole realm of nature mine
> That were a present far too small.
> Love so amazing, so divine
> Demands my soul, my life, my all.
> —Isaac Watts

Though the servant poem is a drama picturing an ideal, in Jesus Christ this dream became a reality. Christ rules from the cross which has become His throne. The two hardest and most unnatural things to do are to say to God "Thy will be done" and to sacrifice self in service for a spiritually destitute world. When, however, we try sincerely to follow the "steps of His wounded feet," we too will find victory, "divide the spoil with the strong," and attain a portion with those who are truly great.

10
Nevermore to Roam
(54:1 to 55:13)

Someone has defined a good sermon or any other message as consisting of a good introduction and a good conclusion, not too far apart. Whatever basis you use for outlining the Book of Isaiah, and whomever you consider to be the author of the several parts, one thing is certain. Chapters 40—55 stand as a literary unit and could well have existed as a separate roll with an independent circulation for a period of time before being incorporated into the larger book just as many of Jeremiah's various components. The two chapters we are now considering conclude and climax this section.

Analysis of Two Chapters

The oracles of consolation which began at 49:14 were interrupted twice. In 50:4-11, the prophet pictured the Lord's Servant made perfect through His sufferings while in 52:13 to 53:12 the prophet showed the means by which deliverance would come to the people. Though in some ways 52:13 to 53:12 and chapter 54 differ, they actually deal with the same subject but from two distinct standpoints. The first describes the inward process of conversion that makes the nation righteous while the second presents the salvation which results. The glowing benefits pictured in chapter 54 are the spillover from the prophet's contemplation of the Suffering Servant's work. On the other hand, chapter 55 issues an invitation for Israel to take the salvation offered and concludes with a reaffirmation of the Lord's sovereignty and His determination to implement His plan for world redemption through Israel.

Excitement of Returning Home

Do you recall the thrill of "going home day" when you had been on an extended trip for business reasons, a hospitalization, or even a vacation? An old cliché says that the best part of going away is coming home. Multiply that by seventy years, hundreds of miles, and thousands of people and we can begin to realize the feeling of the exiles. In chapter 40, we read where the prophet said of Israel, "her warfare is accomplished . . . her iniquity is pardoned . . . she hath received . . . double for all her sin" (40:2). In 54:1, the implementation of the Lord's promise was about to begin. If the song had been written in their day, the Israelites might well have sung as they prepared and as they began to march

> [We've] wandered far away from God
> Now [we're] coming home
> The paths of sin too long we've trod
> Lord, [we're] coming home.
>
> Coming home, Coming home,
> Never more to roam;
> Open wide thine arms of love,
> Lord, [we're] coming home.
> —William J. Kirkpatrick

This is what these last two chapters are all about. The prophet is proclaiming God's promise of peace and prosperity (54:1-17), God's plea for participation (55:1-7), and God's pronouncement of purpose (55:8-13).

I. Promise of Peace and Prosperity (54:1-17)

In "The Vicar of Wakefield," Oliver Goldsmith asked and answered a striking question concerning a woman's unfaithfulness.

> When lovely woman stoops to folly,
> And finds too late that men betray,
> What charm can soothe her melancholy?
> What art can wash her guilt away?
>
> The only art her guilt to cover,
> To hide her shame from every eye,
> To give repentance to her lover,
> And wring his bosom, is—to die.

The prophet followed Hosea's figure of speech as he addressed the nation about to return home. Though Israel was the Lord's servant, she was also the one whom He had chosen centuries earlier to be His bride. She had not been faithful, but He refused to cast her off.

Wife to Be Honored

A threefold command articulates the joy that Israel should feel. As long as she was in Exile, she could not produce children to further God's redemptive plan, but He had stooped not to point the finger of scorn at her but to show mercy and comfort to the one He had chosen in her soul's vexation. All three verbs in the first verse are picturesque, but the third, usually translated "cry aloud" is actually the word used for a horse's neighing. A "shrill cry of joy" is perhaps the best meaning in this context. Such expressions as "jump for joy" and "act with hilarity" have also been suggested. The Lord had redeemed His people and was about to breathe new life into them. How could they refuse to be jubilant?

When people use a figure of speech, we cannot always force a strictly logical consistency upon them. Scholars have not agreed entirely, but most feel the "desolate wife" is the nation while in Exile and the "married wife" is the nation before the captivity. Yet the desolate wife was about to be restored to favor. No longer would she be barren, humiliated, forsaken by her husband, storm-tossed, and comfortless. The Lord would bring His bride in triumphant love and once again she would produce children to implement His redemptive program. In fact, even though she did not realize it, she already had more children, and they were waiting to be acknowledged by the Lord.

Prepare for Increase!

For this reason, the Lord told Zion to get ready for an "expansion program." The prophet used the figure of a tent, and Edward J. Young suggested the symbolic thought of Zion dwelling in her tent as Rebekah was carried by Isaac into his mother's tent (Gen. 24:67) and Laban went into the tents of Jacob, Leah, and Rachel, looking for his stolen gods (Gen. 31:34). Young contended also that the figure suggested the "Church has no permanent abode in this world but is like a nomad travelling from place to place until she comes to her final and enduring abode, the heavenly city." The place of the tent could have been either the room within the tent or the place upon which the tent was erected. The curtains were the cloth stretched from one pole to the other to form the tent. The cords were the ropes that tied the tent to the stakes driven into the ground. Zion must obey these commands, not retrenching but preparing for great posterity. Too much could not be done to make the tents roomier because the Lord had promised a large increase.

Another factor, however, must not be forgotten. Increased extension demands a corresponding increase of stability. Any camper who is familiar with tents recognizes the prophet's figure immediately. When you pitch a tent, if you lengthen the ropes, you must strengthen the stakes. The prophet spoke to our own day in this message in a very significant way. Before we move out in effective spiritual service, we must be certain that our own personal experience with the Lord is a valid one. As we enter new areas of growth, we must not forget the fundamentals of the faith. Likewise, a Christian denomination must never feel it can continue numerical expansion by ignoring or watering down the original beliefs and convictions that made it strong in the first place.

Restored Israel would spread numerically and possess the nations. The true fulfillment of this promise, however, was not found in political expansion and national growth but in the spread of the Christian gospel as spiritual Israel, those who became believers in Jesus Christ, took the message of redemption and salvation to the nations.

Past to Be Forgotten

Knowing that the joy and fruitfulness of the new relationship would be so great that the dark unhappy days of the past would be forgotten, the prophet gave Israel a twofold assurance. First, the shame of her youth, her early days as a nation, the reproach of her widowhood, and the horrible experiences during the Babylonian Exile would vanish from her memory. For this reason, she had no need to fear or feel frustrated in any way. The Hebrew text reads literally, "Thy husband, thy maker," emphasizing the intimate relationship God felt toward Israel. The prophet pointed to the future when the one God of the universe would be recognized specifically by His moral and ethical characteristics. He would be to every person the Ever-Living One in charge of the heavenly forces, the God of holy character, and most of all the One who delighted to forgive those who were overtaken by sin.

How could the Lord wed Himself to such an obscure group of people? This was indeed the secret of Israel's destiny. Further, it was the source of both her humiliation and her glory. God must punish sin because of His holiness, but He delights to forgive because of His mercy. Israel's past transgressions and sufferings will seem as nothing when forgiveness comes. Hugh Black told of how a man he knew felt remorse every time he passed a certain house because of sins in his early life connected with the house. The shame was almost unbearable until he gave his life to Jesus Christ and experienced the personal forgiveness that comes with such a surrender. He testified that his soul was filled by a great transport of joy that the sins of the past were no longer a part of his life because God had "forgiven and forgotten" and cast them behind His back.

God's Presence Guaranteed

The "overflowing wrath" of which the prophet spoke in verse 8 perhaps called to his mind the deluge in Noah's day, and he used it as an illustration of how strong and unconditional was His promise to be with the people as they returned home. In Noah's day when the flood was over, God swore He would never again in His wrath overwhelm His creation by such a deluge. Now, He made a similar promise to those He had chosen to bring His salvation to the world. Since mountains and hills were the most permanent things Israel knew of, God used them to illustrate the everlasting quality of His love for the nation. His covenant to use them in bringing redemption and peace to the nations would outlast these things that Israel considered most indestructible.

A New Jerusalem

In order to reinforce His promise, the prophet made a fresh start by addressing the city with descriptive phrases that revealed the depth of woe she had suffered and was still feeling though her redemption was nigh. The poor, ruined capital city of Judah on her forlorn hilltop was promised future external glory. The vision of the New Jerusalem with its walls, foundations, battle towers, gates, and extended possessions all reflecting earthly glory give us a foregleam of the heavenly city in the Book of Revelation. Both men spoke for people who lived in dark times when survival of God's people seemed impossible. They encouraged their people to have faith by setting before them the vision of a holy city in which evil no longer had any power, and God's ethical righteousness would guarantee an environment where nothing could disturb nor threaten.

Outward Splendor

The word pictures used in describing the external magnificence of the city are appealing. The term used to describe that in which the stones of the wall would be set is difficult to translate. One scholar said it refers to a black mineral powder used as an eye pigment. Another thought it may have been similar to a substance Arab women use even today and was mixed with a liquid to make a cement or paste. Another student suggested the prophet referred not merely to the stones of the city walls, but to every stone of the city. He even went so far as to claim every stone would appear like the decorated eye of a woman. Some people's literalism knows no bounds!

The phrase "lay thy foundations" reads literally "will found thee" while the noun *sapphire* comes from a verb root which means to write, number, or count. No one is certain as to the exact meaning of the Hebrew word. Our English word *sapphire* means a precious stone of transparent rich blue mineral. Franz Delitzsch suggested the blue of sapphire is the "color of heaven, of revelation, and of the covenant." God will give the renewed Zion her heavenly beauty that He alone can give.

The word translated "pinnacles" comes from a word which means "sun" but, in the plural, means "windows" or "notched battlements." One translation renders it "towers" (GNB) while another translates "minarets." The word rendered "carbuncle," a word defined in English as "any of several red precious stones," comes from a Hebrew verb root which means "to kindle" or "to burn." The literal Hebrew reads "thy gate stones of Carbuncles." In the next phrase, the same word is used for "stones" and the same grammatical form is used with a word that means "delight," "pleasure," or "preciousness." The word rendered "border" means "boundary" or "limited space." A good translation for the phrase would be "all thy territory, precious stones."

Spiritual Quality

The cumulative effect of this highly figurative description of the new Jerusalem is that of outward splendor. This would of course appeal to the materialistic-minded person even as the description of the New Jerusalem in the Book of Revelation appeals to those who are looking for heaven to be a place of literal wealth and earthly possessions, transplanted to a celestial city. The prophet went on, however, to emphasize the spiritual qualities of life in the restored capital of Judah. Two things would characterize the city's inner life. First, the inhabitants would be "learners," taught by God Himself. In the New Testament, spiritual Zion or the New Israel was made up of those who were disciples of Christ. This group was called "Christians" at Antioch (Acts 11:26). Followers of Jesus have been primarily called by that name since that time. How beautifully the "New is in the Old concealed, and the Old is in the New revealed!" Such people have within their hearts a calmness that enables them to be whole personalities. This is the essence of God's kingdom—His rule within the human heart. Second, the foundation stone of city life will be ethical integrity. The word *righteousness* occurs first in the Hebrew text in verse 14, emphasizing its importance. The word stands for just deeds, guaranteeing equity to the people but also indicating the right relationship with God which is both the cause and effect of such actions.

Love Conquers Hate

Beginning with the second phrase in verse 14, the prophet gave his final word to Israel in this section of Scripture. The first verb should be rendered as an imperative: keep "far from oppression." Knowing that practicing justice would make her strong, the prophet urged Israel to offer the peoples of the earth God's redemptive love. In this way, she could best hope to be free from oppression from them. As a modern cliche says, "The best way to be free from your enemy's attack is to love him to death" or "Kiss your enemies and make them your friends." In this context, the prophet was anticipating one of the greatest New Testament truths. In bringing new life to others, Israel would find fullness of life for herself. Jesus said, "For whosoever would save his life shall lose it: and whosoever shall lose his life for my sake shall find it" (Matt. 16:25).

Although spiritual conquest is the best way to be free from an enemy's attack, the prophet promised the people that they would be protected from those who refused to live by God's righteous principles. If they did assemble against Israel, God would have no part in it as He did when He made Nebuchadnezzar His "servant" to execute His wrath upon the sinful nation that needed to be chastised. He would see to it that Israel would be successful in defending herself if an attack did come.

God's Ability and Resources

How could God give such a promise? He is omnipotent and makes the makers of the weapons. Also, He created the "waster," the one who uses the weapons that destroy. Thus, all the processes of warfare are in His hand. In both cases where the word *I* occurs in verse 16, the pronoun appears separately in the Hebrew text, emphasizing that God Himself did it—I and not someone else!

No one thinks independently of God though people may for a short time think that they do. This does not mean, however, that God can be blamed for the evil that people do in every situation. Verse 15 makes it clear that those who might plan to do evil against Israel would not plot this wickedness because of God's initiative. God does of course at times raise up people as instruments of His anger, but this does not make Him responsible for every cruel human deed.

Nothing Can Harm God's People

No weapon that would be formed against Israel would prosper (v. 17). The Hebrew text expresses it a bit differently, "Every weapon formed against thee will not prosper." This means they will not succeed in their design or purpose. Likewise, no formal accusation against Israel would succeed. Israel would be able to answer all who bring any charges against her for misconduct or unfairness in dealing with people. This applied of course as long as she stayed with God's laws of righteousness and equity. The "tongue" represents the accuser rather than the irresponsible gossiper. Both from weapons and formal charges, Israel would be safe and victorious over those who sought to hurt her.

The final "saith Jehovah" affirms not only the immediately preceding promises but every one in the address that began at the first verse of the chapter. The prophetic formula promised that all the resources of God would be used if necessary to bring peace and prosperity to the people as they returned home. James D. Smart said, "God reigns and his purpose will ultimately be fulfilled. Evil, however mighty as it may seem, will be overthrown." God has spoken, and He will bring it to pass!

II. Plea to Participate (55:1-7)

Chapter 54 resembles the Book of Revelation in that it envisions the New Jerusalem and describes the people who will populate it. Chapter 55 resembles the Book of John as it appeals to the people to open their eyes to the rich gifts God offers so freely and urges them while opportunity remains to grasp these blessings through repentance and faith. This invitation seems directed more to individual Israelites than to the nation as a whole. We must never forget that God always worked with the spiritual nucleus, the Israel within Israel, to accomplish His purposes in history.

An Evangelistic Appeal

The Babylonian Exile left indelible marks upon the Israelites. Living in the midst of a great trading center, they developed that business expertise which has characterized them through the centuries. Though restrictions were placed upon them, they were allowed to mingle with the people and engage in commercial transactions. Some no doubt prospered and lost the desire to return home. Others, however, remained homesick and longed for those things that money cannot buy. God through the prophet spoke to them of the imperishable things of the Spirit and urged them to participate in His redemptive program for the nations rather than remaining in Babylon and becoming more absorbed in material things.

This section sounds like a revival meeting invitation as the prophet issued an altar call urging the people to come to God's great salvation. He couched his message in symbolic terms, but all the essentials of New Testament salvation by grace were present. As the symphonic drama unfolded, redemption had been presented (52:13 to 53:12), and the promise for peace and prosperity had been added (54:1-17). Now God sent forth a cry for them to become involved. Ten imperatives are found in the first three verses, but they should be considered kind urgings rather than sharp commands. He did not try to compel the people but respected their personhood and left them room to refuse.

Spiritual Values Paramount

Events related to the Exodus from Egypt and journeying to the Promised Land were connected with eating and drinking. The covenant God made with Israel at Sinai was sealed with a feast (Ex. 24:11). During the wilderness wanderings, she witnessed His providential concern for her sustenance. Even when He described the delights of Canaan, He spoke of it as "a land flowing with milk and honey." God reminded the people, however, that the ultimate values are spiritual as He said that He fed them with manna that they might learn "man does not live on bread alone but on every word that comes from the mouth of the Lord" (Deut. 8:3, NIV).

Moving from the imperative mode, the prophet used a question to point out to Israel the folly of rejecting God's offer of salvation and concentrating all her attention and energy on accumulating things that bring no happiness. The water, wine, milk, and bread offered to Israel were not gifts of God apart from Himself but rather were symbols of life in Him. Water flowing in the desert spoke of God coming into the barren and unproductive places of the human life. Wine symbolized exilaration and enjoyment while milk meant nourishment. Bread stood for the basic fact of one's existence. Without it, no life was possible. The biblical emphasis of salvation is always on the qualitative nature of both the relationship and the fellowship in the Lord it brings. The prophet did, however, offer prosperity, which is the Hebrew concept of "fatness," if they would "eat . . . that which is good." When one makes right choices in the moral realm, he lives the kind of life that God can bless with material prosperity though we must remember that sometimes righteous people suffer hardships in spite of their good deeds.

The Covenant and the Messiah

The prophet returned to the "command format" (v. 3), promising not only a vitality of life if the people listened to God's way, but also a continuing part in the covenant that He had made with the nation. We must be careful in drawing fine distinctions between the various times that God made covenants with different people. The basic promise of God since the Eden experience was that He would bring His redemptive program to fruition. Along the way, He used various individuals as well as the nation Israel. Of course, we look to God's covenant with Abraham as the beginning of His redemptive program through the Jewish people, but in a unique way David stood out as a symbol of the coming Messiah. Though some scholars have gone to great length in discussing the latter part of verse 3, the prophet seemed to be saying simply that if Israel would be faithful God will use her in implementing the redemptive program He initiated long ago and had symbolized most vividly in David.

When the prophet spoke of David as a witness, he did not mean this in the sense of one who gave testimony in court but that David would by his life and words proclaim God's truth to the nations. David did this, and Israel as a nation was to continue this noble mission. Edward J. Young saw the words "leader" (or "prince") and "commander" as designating David's position and his work. Thus in the three descriptive words, *witness, leader,* and *commander* (v. 4), we see two functions of the Messiah: prophet and king.

Though the word *nation* is in the singular form both times in verse 5, the plural verb is used in connection with it the second time, causing many scholars to see the noun as plural or at least having a collective use which implies many nations will come to Israel because of her work as the Lord's servant. The peoples of the world would recognize that no other God exists, and their devotion must be given to Him for He alone is worthy of their worship. This was of course fulfilled ultimately in Jesus Christ and the spread of His gospel to the nations.

An Urgent Plea

After the glorious declaration of Israel's extended influence, the prophet returned to his plea for the people to participate. This time, the note of urgency was sounded. We should not, however, restrict this invitation to Israel or to any time frame. This is a universal and timeless call to everyone, everywhere to come to the Lord while He is available. The word *seek* means more than sacrifice or even prayer. The basic idea of the word is "to tread," and the act of seeking God means stepping to God or simply coming to Him.

The words *seek* and *call upon* (v. 6) are parallel expressions, and the next verse shows that repentance is not only involved in the experience but is a basic part of the spiritual transaction. The old way of life must be completely abandoned, and a whole-souled turning to God must take place in genuine humility. Repentance was indeed the first step of a lifelong process of taking God's attitude toward sin.

No mention is made in this context of idolatry. Earlier, the prophet had "laughed out of court" both it and the idol makers. To the prophet, sin was something far more terrible than idolatry, having shown in chapter 53 what wicked people will do to the Servant when they are left to their own devices. He saw sin as planning one's own affairs and pursuing one's course relentlessly in self-centered disregard for the plan that the Lord has revealed. God, however, has always had compassion. Even as far back as the Garden of Eden, He took fallen man and woman in all their pitiable emptiness and with merciful love He gave them clothes to cover their nakedness. Forgiveness is always offered to people even before they are aware of their need for it. Each person, however, must of his own free will "turn" and come back to the Lord in repentance. An ancient Egyptian psalm has been discovered which says, "if the servant is ready to trespass, the Lord is ready to be gracious." How different is our gospel, both in the Old and New Testaments. Only repentance "to the uttermost" can save one from self destruction. Though he spoke in love, the prophet made clear God's requirement, and it is the climax of this section.

III. Pronouncement of Purpose (55:8-13)

The symphonic drama which began with words of comfort to the exiles that they had suffered sufficiently for their sin (40:1-2) concludes with a threefold affirmation that included a statement of God's complete superiority to the people (vv. 8-9), an assurance that no declaration of God would fail but rather will accomplish His purpose (vv. 10-11), and a picture of the final victory when joy will come to those align themselves with His purpose for world redemption. A definite break comes in the prophet's message at the close of chapter 55. Chapters 40—55 stand as a separate literary unit, written by a spiritual genius and inbreathed by God Himself. No portion of Scripture in the Old Testament shows more clearly the presence of God's Spirit than these sixteen chapters.

Man Cannot Fathom God

The fact that God's thoughts and ways cannot be identified with man's cannot be limited to any one aspect of truth. Certainly, the contrast between divine holiness and human sinfulness comes to our mind immediately. Not only the Book of Isaiah but the entire Old Testament trumpets forth the fact that a great gulf exists between the moral purity of Israel's God and the wickedness of the people. Likewise, the people are urged to be holy because their God is holy. Also, we find in these verses an anticipation of the Kierkegaardian principle that the finite cannot comprehend the infinite. The prophet's main thrust in this context, however, concerns God's redemptive program. Persons fail to see the great desire on God's part to forgive sinful people and create a new community of believers who will reflect the holiness of their God and will spread the message of His accessibility to the nations. George A. F.

Knight said that "man cannot even begin to comprehend the depths and heights of the love of God and of his plans of salvation that embrace the whole of creation." To compare the Babylonian, bowed down with superstitions, riddled with jealousies and fears, and filled with bestial and repulsive morals, to Israel's God approximated the distinction between heaven and earth. God's purposes in redemption are indeed too sublime to be measured or even understood by sinful and despairing minds.

God's Plans Succeed

Moving from this great contrast, the prophet next showed with the aid of a lengthy simile that what God has declared contains a self-fulfilling energy and would take place even as He had proclaimed. In verse 10, the prophet introduced the rain and snow as agents of God in producing food for consumption. He said that they "returneth not thither, but watereth the earth." The emphasis, however, is not on the fact that they do not return but rather that they accomplish their intended purpose. The food that grows for us is the inevitable outcome of God's loving purpose for people in the processes of nature. The movement cannot reverse itself but must go forward according to the pattern God has created, one that reveals His love. The pattern is effective for it results in fulfilling the divine purpose.

The prophet then stated the analogy by which he proclaimed the certainty of God's redemptive plan. When God speaks, He does so with intent. Salvation is His purpose, and in His word resides divine power which will transform the earth from chaos into a Kingdom of justice and peace. The prophet knew that the people knew the Word of God had been sent forth. The ultimate fulfillment would not come until this Word became flesh in the birth of our Savior. Even in the prophet's day, however, the spoken word contained a power that made it irresistible, guaranteeing success and victory for God's purposes in history. Edward J. Young pointed out that though in this context the element of blessing seems to predominate, the thought is not limited to that truth. The word is not only effective for bringing salvation but also for condemning the wicked. In the New Testament, we find the words of Jesus recorded that "the word that I spake, the same shall judge him in the last day" (John 12:48). The "shall accomplish" and "shall prosper" (v. 11) are prophetic perfects with the latter being in the causative stem and translated properly "make to prosper."

In His Own Time

A word of practical observation needs to be made at this point. God does not always reward the righteous and condemn the wicked immediately even though His Word says that they will receive that which is due them. The prophets took the long-range viewpoint. God will vindicate the righteous and punish the wicked when He decides the time is right. We must not attempt to do His work for Him. He says, "Vengeance belongeth unto me: I will recompense" (Rom. 12:19). Not who is ahead in a particular inning of a baseball game determines the winner but who is ahead when the game is completed.

In 1929, a bitterly fought World Series occured between the Chicago Cubs and the Philadelphia Athletics. The Cubs jumped to an early lead and continued to pile up runs. At the middle of the eighth inning, they led 8-0. A phenomenal thing took place that Saturday afternoon. The Athletics scored ten runs in the last of the eighth inning. This so broke the back of the Cubs that they did not score in the top of the ninth, and the Athletics did not even have to take their bat in the ninth inning.

Sometimes God seems to be losing the battle, and sin appears to be in control as wicked people go unpunished. God's Word will win, however, because He stands behind it with all the resources of the divine Godhead. We can trust God to make things right because He has promised that He will and has done so many times in history. Likewise, the prophet insisted that Israel could rest assured, as she stood of the eve of returning home that God would direct and protect her. He had promised and would not allow His word to be defeated.

The Final Redemption

Verses 12-13 end the symphony! Traditionally, these verses have been interpreted as describing the return from Babylon. This is of course the immediate thrust of the prophet's words. More, however, was involved. James Smart spoke of them as "describing the great restoration that is to take place in the day of redemption when God will gather his people from the ends of the earth." He insisted that for the chapter to have a universal outlook in its earlier part with Israel as witness, leader, and commander to all the nations and then end with merely a description of the Exodus from Babylon would be unlikely. It makes good sense! God's purpose in redemption encompasses the whole earth and has as its goal a blessing for all people everywhere.

All of nature would join in and be blessed by God as the Jews moved toward home. Peace would be theirs in the new venture. The expression "peace" means being undisturbed by enemies and also a full trust, confidence, and satisfaction in God who would lead His people home. Obstacles would not hinder them. The mountains and hills, usually hindrances because they must be crossed, are pictured symbolically by the prophet as breaking out into a ringing cry of joy, taking part in the glory of the return of God's people. Even the trees would "clap their hands" as they rejoiced at God's redemptive work. Rather than creation groaning and travailing in pain, as it has since Eden, it shall be liberated when God's plan for world redemption is consummated.

Human Nature Changed

The final symbol pictures the fir tree replacing the thorn and the myrtle replacing the brier. What better description of that which happens to human nature when transformed by the Lord! Why did Jesus come? To make a new world? Of course! He does it, however, by making new people or better yet by making people new. The Lord did not come so much to create a new society as He did to create the creators of a new society.

The thorns and briers are always with us—sharp, cruel, useless things that make life miserable and unproductive. So many things tear and wound, bringing pain. These frustrating and destructive things will not merely be rooted up but shall be crowded out as the lovely things flourish. The thorn and the brier represent sin and selfishness while the fir and the myrtle are symbols of holiness and sacrifice. No room for evil when righteousness comes! No room for Satan when the Lord enters one's life! The fir and myrtle shall sink their roots deep into the ground, drawing their nutritive forces into a finer and stronger life. Reaching upward toward the sun, they shall drink its warmth into their whole being. The thorns and briers, however, shall find no food for their hungry roots nor sunshine for their prickly branches.

God's Kingdom Is Forever

In ancient days, conquerors often set up memorials to preserve their name and tell of their work to future generations. Their boastings, however, have almost always been destroyed or their recorded vanities have become blurred like the inscriptions at the mouth of the Dog River in

Syria. No later monarch, however, would ever undo the work of Israel's God through His Servant the Messiah—Jesus Christ, our Savior and Lord. In Christ, we have a kingdom that cannot be destroyed because God is One who shakes the things that can be shaken in order that those things which cannot be shaken may remain (Heb. 12:27-28).

God's "everlasting sign that shall not be cut off" is His Kingdom of redeemed people who shall never perish. What a climax for this great symphony! The prophet by divine inspiration certainly spoke more than the people of his day understood, probably more than he himself comprehended, but in Jesus Christ we can see these wonderful truths! May we ever rejoice in and live in the light of them!

Summary of Complete Work

What is the overall message of Isaiah 40—55? Of all the themes that move in and out as the symphony rolls along, one predominates. God's kingdom is coming! We realize that we will never see a perfect world until the kingdom is consummated at the Lord's second coming. We must, however, be Christian optimists, believing that we can help His kingdom to come on earth as we preach the gospel and minister in the name of our Lord. The victory is assured. We need a rekindling of faith and hope as we witness. God's Word will prosper, as the prophet said, when it is sent forth. Though we grow discouraged at times when we see evil winning, we must believe that God is in control of all forces in the universe. When the eyes of Elisha's servant were opened, he saw the "mountain ablaze with horses and chariots of fire." Likewise, we have forces at work for us that, though invisible, are real.

God's kingdom cannot be stopped by temporary defeats in smaller areas. A woman who had spent much time observing the sea learned a great lesson and applied it to the certain progress of God's work in this world of which we are a part. With keen insight, she wrote:

> On the far reef, the breakers
>   Recoil in shattered foam,
> While still the sea behind them
>   Urges its forces home.
> Its song of triumph surges
>   Through all the thunderous din—
> The waves may break in failure
>   But the tide is sure to win!

....
O mighty sea! Thy message
In clanging spray is cast;
Within God's plan of progress
It matters not at last
How wide the shores of evil,
How strong the reefs of sin
The wave may be defeated
But the tide is sure to win!
—Priscilla Leonard

The prophet foresaw a time when, through the work of God's Servant, the kingdoms of this world would become the kingdom of our Lord. How wonderful that we in our day, as the prophet in his, can give ourselves to making that marvelous redemptive purpose of God become a reality in history. Let us never grow weary in well doing, knowing that in God's time we shall reap if we faint not.